ROMW
VERSUS
RAMB

REVEALS,
GOD, ADAM, AND CREATION

ROMW VERSUS RAMB

REVEALS, GOD, ADAM, AND CREATION

SIMEON W. JOHNSON

PRIMIX
PUBLISHING
THE WRITE CHOICE

Primix Publishing
11620 Wilshire Blvd
Suite 900, West Wilshire Center, Los Angeles, CA, 90025
www.primixpublishing.com
Phone: 1 (888) 585-7476

© 2021 Simeon W. Johnson. All rights reserved.

No part of this book may be reproduced, stored in a retrieval system, or transmitted by any means without the written permission of the author.

All scripture quotations, unless otherwise noted, have been taken from the Holy Bible, King James Version.

Published by Primix Publishing   04/10/2021

ISBN: 978-1-955177-04-7(sc)
ISBN: 978-1-955177-05-4(e)

Library of Congress Control Number: 2021907970

Any people depicted in stock imagery provided by iStock are models, and such images are being used for illustrative purposes only.

Certain stock imagery © iStock.

Because of the dynamic nature of the Internet, any web addresses or links contained in this book may have changed since publication and may no longer be valid. The views expressed in this work are solely those of the author and do not necessarily reflect the views of the publisher, and the publisher hereby disclaims any responsibility for them.

CONTENTS

A Tribute to Black America ix

Chapter 1.   Creation versus Evolution, Fact or Fiction? 1
Chapter 2.   The First Birth Pain of the Human Race 15
Chapter 3.   Creation versus Man's Declaration of
             Independence from His Creator 29
Chapter 4.   The Best Cure for AIDS. 40
Chapter 5.   He Loves Us like No Other 44
Chapter 6.   The Battle of the Will versus the Chastening of
             the Enemy 51
Chapter 7.   Our Unique Earth 56
Chapter 8.   Hominid Fills Gap in Fossil Record 62
Chapter 9.   Human Love versus Instinctive Love in the
             Animal Species. 68
Chapter 10. Wisdom versus Philosophy. 73
Chapter 11. The Increase of Knowledge 84
Chapter 12. The Significance of the Speed of Thought 93

About the Author 103

In honor of my beloved mother who passed away much too soon.

You were blessed to see the youngest of your ten sons grow up to be a man!

Nevertheless, just as the family tree of our first parents,
so does our family tree continue.
May your soul rest in peace.

A TRIBUTE TO BLACK AMERICA

The following is a true story of Black America's contribution toward the building of this great nation. I obtained this information while visiting Pastor Dennis's church in Brooklyn, New York, on Sunday, February 27, 2000. The reading of this article by a young lady of the church youth group inspired me immensely as offers of free copies were given to everyone who wanted it. I requested a copy from the youth leader with permission to share this information with others.

Although I have just completed the manuscript of my second book, a thought that came to mind. What better way for me to make a contribution to this country than to share this information with others in my book! Therefore, I will take this opportunity to interject this appropriate response to a statement made by a well-known radio and TV show. An opinionated talk show host made a challenge to anyone who could show him where Black America has ever made any meaningful contribution to the building of this great nation. For that reason—and to all concerned—here are the facts!

This is a story of a little boy named Theo who woke up one morning, and asked his mother, "Mom, what if there were no black people in the world?"

Well, his mother thought about that for a moment, and then said, "Son, follow me around today. Let's just see what it would be like if there were no black people in the world. Now go get dressed and we will get started." Theo ran to his room to put on his clothes and shoes.

His mother took one look at him and said, "Theo, where are your shoes? And those clothes are all wrinkled, son, I must iron them." But when she reached for the ironing board, it was no longer there. You see, Sarah Boon, a black woman, invented the ironing board, and Jan Ernst Matzeliger, a black man, invented the shoe lacing machine! "Oh well," she said. "Please go and do something to your hair."

Theo ran to his room to comb his hair, but the comb was not there. You see, Elroy J. Duncan, a black man, invented the comb. Theo decided to just brush his hair, but the brush was gone. Well, this was a sight—no shoes, wrinkled clothes, hair a mess even his mom's hair, without the hair care inventions of Madam C. J. Walker…well, you get the picture.

Mom told Theo, "Let's do our chores around the house and then take a trip to the grocery store."

Theo's job was to sweep the floor. When he reached for the dustpan, it was not there. You see, Lloyd P. Ray, a black man, invented the dustpan. So he swept his pile of dirt over in the corner and left it there. He then decided to mop the floor, but the mop was gone. You see, Thomas W. Stewart, a black man, invented the mop. Theo yelled to his "Mom! Mom, I'm not having any luck!"

"Well, son," she said, "let me finish washing these clothes then we will prepare a list for the grocery store. When she was finished, she went to put the clothes in the dryer, but it was not there. You see, George T. Sampson, a black man, invented the clothes dryer.

Mom asked Theo to get a pencil and some paper to prepare them list for the market. Theo ran to get them, but noticed the pencil lead was broken. He was out of luck because John Lee Love, a black man, invented the pencil sharpener. When Mom reached for a pen, it was not there because William Purvis, a black man, invented the fountain pen. The truth is, Lee Brundige invented the typewriting machine and W. A. Lovette invented the advanced printing press.

Theo and his mother decided to head out to the market. When Theo opened the door, he noticed the grass was as high as he was tall. You see, the lawn mower was invented by John Burr, a black man. They made their way over to the car and found that it just wouldn't start. You see, Richard B. Spikes, a black man, invented automatic gear shift and Joseph Gammel invented the supercharge system for internal combustion engines. They noticed that the few cars that were moving were crashing into each other because there were no traffic signals. You see, Garret A. Morgan, a black man, invented the traffic lights.

Well, it was getting late so they walked to the market, got their groceries, and returned home. Just when they were about to put away the milk, eggs, and butter, they noticed the refrigerator was gone. You see, John Standard, a black man, invented the refrigerator. So they just left the food on the counter. By this time, Theo noticed he was getting mighty cold. He went to turn up the heat. And what do you know! Alice Parker, a black female, invented the heating furnace. Even in the summertime, they would have been out of luck because Fredrick Jones, a black man, invented the air conditioner.

It was almost time for Theo's father to arrive home. He usually takes the bus, but there was no bus because its precursor was the electric trolley, which was invented by another black man, Elbert R. Robinson. He usually takes the elevator from his office on the twentieth floor, but there was no elevator because Alexander Miles, a black man, invented it. He also usually dropped off the office mail at a nearby mailbox, but it was no longer there because Philip B. Downing, a black man, invented the letter drop mailbox and William Barry invented the postmarking and canceling machine. Theo and his mother sat at the kitchen table with their head in their hand. When the father arrived, he asked, "Why are you sitting in the dark?" Lewis Howard Latimer, a black man, invented the filament within the light bulb.

Theo quickly learned what it would be like if there were no black people in the world. Not to mention that if he ever got sick and needed blood, Charles Drew, a black scientist, found a way to preserve and store blood, which led to his starting the world's first blood bank. What if a family member had to have heart surgery? This would not have been possible without Dr. Daniel Hale Williams, a black doctor who performed the first open-heart surgery!

So if you ever wonder, like Theo, it's plain to see we would still be in the dark!

- Facts

If there were no black people, there wouldn't be a lot of things. There wouldn't be traffic lights, mailboxes, combs, brushes, etc..

- Comment

"If there weren't any black people, a lot of things might not have been invented!" I learned that black people, in particular, have been and will always be a great asset to America and all the people of the world.

- Peculiarity

The dictionary defines peculiarity as:

- character of only one,
- strange,
- something inherent and distinctive, etc.

This reminds me of the story of a man who was having a social conversation with his wife when the statement of peculiarity was called into question. The husband turned to his wife and said, "I think everyone is a little peculiar, except me and *thee*, and sometimes I think *thee* is a little peculiar too!"

The moral of the story is, no matter who we are—whether Jew or Gentile, Catholic or Protestant—we were all created in the image of our Creator. All our works and contributions to society, whether as free men or women, or bond slaves, we all will be rewarded for the good works as well as for the evil work. Being peculiar, however, does not give anyone the right to point the finger at the inferior states of another race. Just remember, while you are pointing the finger at others, the other fingers are pointing back at you. Therefore, those who publicly question whether or not black America had ever made any meaningful contribution toward the development of this great country, you would be well advised to research and learn from the information presented in this narrative.

Simeon Johnson

1
CREATION VERSUS EVOLUTION, FACT OR FICTION?

I attempt this arduous task of defending the evidence of the creation of this magnificent earth and the universe by an intelligent Creator, the Maker of heaven and earth. This belief is espoused by millions of Bible-believing Christians throughout the history of the human race, a statement of fact not without its critics ever since the beginning of time. Despite the vicious assault forged against our beliefs, at the end of all things, the truth will be vindicated!

Since time began, man has always tried to eradicate the faith of the people of God with every imaginable atrocity ever devised—to no avail, thank God. A recent headline reads, "How Man Evolved Amazing New Discoveries Reveal the Secrets of our Past: Remarkable New Evidence Is Filling in the Story of How We Became Human."

With all due respect, however, I categorically refute the evidence of their findings not from a scientific or an intellectual point of view or state of pompous arrogance but from absolute certainty and assurance based on the word of God and a personal relationship with the Lord. For more details, read *From the Brink of Suicide* by Simeon Johnson (Vantage Press Inc., NY, July 1998), a book that is changing lives everywhere! "A life is a precious thing to waste."

The article goes on to say that despite the protest of creationists and intellectuals, "virtually every other type of animal comes in multiple varieties… Even our closest kin, the great apes, fall into four species, divided into several subspecies." That is man's assumption. Nevertheless, the following are the declared words of the Creator:

- "In the beginning, God created heaven and the earth" described in (Genesis chapters 1 through 3),
- "In the beginning was the Word, and the Word was with God, and the Word was God. The same was in the beginning with God. All things were made by him; and without him was not anything made that was made. In him was life; and the life was the light of men. And the light shineth in darkness; and the darkness comprehended it not" (Jn. 1:1–5).

After God formed man out of the dust of the ground and breathed into his nostrils the breath of life, and man became a living soul with body, soul, and spirit, made in the Image of God. He did not evolve from an ape, as the evolutionists falsely alleged.

The article continued to say, "A few million years ago, most of us think, the half-ape known as Lucy appeared in Africa; eventually she begat a less apelike creature, who evolved into something even more humanlike. Finally, after a few more begetting, Homo sapiens appeared." The Neanderthals are commonly seen as offspring "from proto-apes" to modern humans. "The evolution of successful animal species usually involves trial and errors, false starts, and failed experiments. Humans are no exception to this, says anthropologist Ian Tattersall of the American Museum of Natural History in New York City, no matter what we like to think."

So whose report will you believe? The Genesis account of Creation (Genesis chapters 1–3, John 1:1–5), and 1 John 1:1–5) or the flawed account of finite man? Again, the question is asked: Would it be a fair and accurate answer for Adam to answer to the critics of his day? Were you there when God created man in his own image? Arguably, there are those who might struggle over the question and answer given if he had answered yes to his critics. Whether his answer would be true or not, the truth is, before Adam, man was never created. Therefore, whose report will you believe, the book of Genesis or the evolutionist's account of Creation as random selective mutation of life form?

We continue with this discussion of facts or fiction and the awful lies the enemy has perpetrated on the human race. That lying deceiver in the form of a serpent said to the woman, "Yea, hath God said, Ye shall not eat of every tree of the garden?" (Gen. 3:1). Take cognizance of the question that the serpent asked the woman knowing full well that God specifically told Adam and his wife that they might eat of every tree of the garden freely, "But of the tree of the knowledge of good and evil, thou shalt not eat of it: for in the day that thou eatest thereof thou shalt surely die" (Gen. 2:17). Again, notice that God did not say "today" or "this day!" A remarkable contrast from what Christ told the dying thief on the cross when Jesus specifically said, "Today shalt thou be with me in paradise" (Lk. 23:43). Oh, what remarkable assurance knowing that to be absent from the body is to be present with the Lord (2 Cor. 5:8).

Let us continue with the discussion of how Satan distorted the truth in order to deceive the woman in the garden of Eden. Perhaps the serpent was just waiting to see the immediate result of his, Paul's experience, when he was then bitten by a venomous viper, was expected to die from the deadly venom by curious onlookers (Acts 28:3–6).

Fortunately for Adam, his wife, and their offspring, although they did not experience physical death after disobeying God's commandment concerning the forbidden fruit. They did, however, die spiritually the very moment sin entered their lives. Christ, being the Lamb slain before the foundation of the world, through his marvelous grace of love and forgiveness has foiled the tempters' plan by denying Satan the victory. The irrevocable curse pronounced upon the serpent was explicit. God categorically told the serpent, "Thou art cursed" (Gen. 3:14). "And I will put enmity between thee and the woman, and between thy seed and her seed; it shall bruise thy head, and thou shalt bruise his heal." At the cross (Lk. 23:46), was buried, and resurrected as our Savior it's a clear-cut reminder to us all that the word of God is real and should not be tampered with. It is permanently embedded into the Scriptures and therefore cannot be erased by any means, period.

ROMW versus RAM Reveals God, Adam and Creation

In the vocabulary of computer language, we have the acronyms ROM and RAM. ROM means read-only memory, which the original designer of the computer software intended not to be modified. Once the plan and method of operation for which it was designed is written permanently in the software program (ROM), there should be no attempt to overwrite or modify its memory. That is why it is so-called read only.

So if man, with his finite knowledge, has designed such clever device and method of operation and made something so unique and cleverly tamper-proof, how vitally important it is for us not to tamper with the superior and flawless design of the Creator of heaven and earth, especially the evolutionist who unlawfully attempts to undermine God's creative work.

The instruction and information encoded into the software program by the designer and programmer of the computer software are written with specific instructions to adhere to by the user and operator of the device. God, who is sovereign Creator and designer of all creations, made it abundantly clear that there should be no tampering with the creative work of God and his written word (Genesis chapters 1–3 and Revelation 22:18–21).

- ROMW

God's spiritual version of read-only my word (ROMW), which means, "read only my word of proclamation, and do not add to or take away from its intended meaning and purpose." So if God's infallible word is so clearly depicted and demonstrated in all of creation, why then does the subversive teachings of Darwinism permeate the hearts and minds of so many people? Why do they believe the doctrine of random selective mutation, a popular belief held by Darwin's theory of evolution?

- RAM

RAM means random access memory", a universal term well known by almost every computer user. The dictionary defines the word *random* as:

1. statistics
2. a phenomenon that does not produce the same outcome every time it occurs under identical circumstances
3. a sample of the population with each member of the population having an equal chance of an event frequently that approaches a stable limit as the number of observations event increase to infinity
4. having no specific pattern or objective, haphazard
5. without a definite method or purpose.

The definitions above, the word *random* means you can read and write the program at will! If I may coin the acronym RAMB, which stands for "random access make-believe," unlike ROM (read-only memory). A program designated by the designer and creator of the software program that was not designed for manipulation by the operator of the device. Despite the ingenuity of man, however, he has his limitations. Despite the fact he can design and control to a certain extent, the activities of RAM and the EEPROM (electrically erasable programmable read-only memory), an acronym I will try to address in more details later in the following chapters.

God, the Creator of all things, made his program ROMW (read-only my word) with his omniscient (all-knowing) intelligence and creative design. Therefore, let no man add to or take away from his written word of the only true account of Creation, not the evolutionist account of random selection of mutation. Thus said the word of God.

The authentic proof of creation is not a make-believe act of the big bang theory, but genuine. Not RAMB, the hypothesis of the Darwin's theory of evolution.

Based on the evidence of the word of God given to us by the holy scripture, it is presumed when the Lord asked Adam, "Where art thou?" we know why they were hiding—because they had sinned and were both naked and afraid so they hid themselves from the presence of the Lord" (Gen. 3:8). Since that time, Adam initiated the first blame game. Through concerted effort, however, they have chosen to live together with whatever conflict they may have encountered by resorting to confiding in each other. However, after God drove them from paradise (the garden of Eden), Adam was ordered to till the ground, and by the sweat of his face, he should eat bread until he returns to the ground. "For out of it wast thou taken: for dust, thou art, and unto dust shalt thou return" (Gen. 3:19).

The Saga of Life's Epic Journey Continues

The first domestic quarrel was initiated the first time after Adam blamed his wife for his own sin. It goes without saying that the same practice is still prevalent in most marriages today. However, like any genuine husband and wife should do, it is written, "for charity shall cover a multitude of sins" (1 Pet. 4:8), because the ties that bind our hearts in Christian love are greater than the conflicts that divide us all. Perhaps, after days, weeks, months, and a number of years went by and there was no evidence of Adam and Eve's physical demise, Satan must have continued to accuse them before God by rehashing his old deception. Referring back to his distorted truth of the question, he originally asked Eve in the garden (Gen. 3:1), he knew exactly what God's command to Adam was the forbidden fruit. However, that was his cunning way of deceiving the woman.

"Be ye therefore wise as serpents, and harmless as doves" (Matt. 10:16). The serpent, as cunning as he is, he is not omniscient. Therefore, he did not know God's original plan of salvation for Adam's fallen race.

Though he has plotted to subvert God's divine plan of salvation from the beginning with his lies and deceptions and ultimately deceived the woman in the garden. His strategies, however, have their limit. The accuser, Lucifer himself has been cast out of heaven, knew how it felt to live in paradise and is determined not to let anyone else experience the joy of heaven. His casting down to earth has reinforced his struggle with God and man to this day.

As Adam struggled with life outside of paradise by tilling the ground and eating bread by the sweat of his face, one cannot begin to imagine how he and his wife must have felt. Oh, the guilt they must have borne knowing they had failed God, their Creator, and destroyed the sacred trust and perfect harmony they once enjoyed in the garden of Eden. No doubt the tempter's accusation must have taken its toll on them because of the tedious life they had to endure. The easy task of caring for the garden, which was a cinch for them in the past, had become a monotonous chore of tilling the ground by the sweat of their brows.

Fatherhood Responsibility

Adam was the first father of the human race, though he had fallen from grace and fellowship with God, his Creator. Prior to his fall when God communed with him and his wife in the cool of the day, God must have taught them all the ways that they should live their lives in the way that is pleasing to him.

We are convinced, however, that Abel was brought up right, his ways pleased God, and his sacrifice was acceptable to him. However, when Cain's sacrifice was rejected, he became angry and slew his brother Abel, the first murder committed of the human race (Gen. 4:8). That must have broken our first parents' hearts, an experience we all can relate to. After the time of bereavement was over, the family union continues to this day, not by random selection of mutation, as the evolutionist would have us to believe, I hasten to add, but rather through the carefully divine salvation, as promised by God the Creator in Genesis 3:15.

After the expulsion from the garden of Eden, Adam toils and labors for his family, which passed through his children and grandchildren. Despite the tedious tasks of tilling the ground by the sweat of his brows to make a living, he must have found some time to enjoy the scenic beauty of God's awesome creation. No doubt he must have enjoyed fishing in the great Euphrates river that flows out of the garden of Eden. Maybe not through the restricted portion that flows directly out of Eden, where he was driven from but in those areas beyond Eden, where the four heads of water diverge from the Garden of Eden and divide into four heads or streams. The Pison went around the land of Havilah where gold was found. The Gihon, which flowed around the whole land of Ethiopia (Cush in Hebrew), the Hiddekel (or Tigris), which flowed in front of Assyria, and the great Euphrates (Gene. 2:8–14).

Living Off the Land

Living off the land, not consciously by choice, but by imperative command, Adam did not have the option to choose or to act upon the right opportunity, nor had the faculty to choose or to decide his future. He had no alternative, but to comply with God's command, to till the ground by the sweat of his brow. This was an imperative and direct command from God, and not a random selection of survival of the fittest, through the process of natural mutation or random selection of the species.

Since Adam and his wife had to live off the land, no doubt, they must have enjoyed eating the different varieties of vegetables, fruits, nuts, and whatever yield or crop the grounds produce. In order to add the necessary proteins to their staple food, Adam must have occasionally added fish to their menu. One would assume, he must have caught fish from the mighty Euphrates. Fortunately, the fish from these waters were not contaminated by the complex combination of amino acids and other bacteria present in living matter, such as mercury and other industrial pollutants. Adam must have taken his sons and grandsons to the river for occasional fishing. Before he sinned, perhaps he could have easily plucked a school of fish from the river without effort. However, after he sinned, the things he had to do were no longer effortless, but tedious and fraught with trials and errors like us imperfect humans. The great river Euphrates, being the longest river, which Israel was acquainted (Gen. 15:18, Deut. 1:7). It makes its rise from two sources in the Armenian mountains, being joined after having run two to 400 miles respectively, through its various branches. Then it flows a thousand miles to the Persian Gulf. The whole course is believed to be 1,700 miles, or 1,200 miles, and said to be navigable for small vessels.

Before Adam and Eve's expulsion from Eden, which, according to Scriptures, believed to be around the land of Havilah where gold was found. By all accounts, it has been said that Adam and Eve lived in that area until they were forced from the garden for eating the forbidden fruit (Genesis chapters 2 and 3). Although the garden has been much investigated, both in ancient and modern times, the mystery of it all is in accordance with the divine plan of the Creator, and not by an act of random mutation as the evolutionist would have us believe. It has been a widely held belief by some scholars who suggested that the district at the head of the Persian Gulf, where the Tigris and the Euphrates rivers flow say it is the oldest civilization found. The generally held belief is that the silt from the river overflowing the bank has added over a hundred miles of land to the head of the gulf since 3000 BC. Though not definitive, its apparent evidence conveys the generally accepted truth. However, the Genesis account of Creation is unquestionable without flaw. According to archaeologists, tablets of clay depict Eden as situated near what was considered that to be ancient shoreline where a sacred palm tree grew. However, I believe the Genesis account.

The Assyrians also mention conquering Eden along with Gozan, Haran, and Rezeph (2 Kgs. 19:12, Isa. 37:12, and Ezek. 27:23). It is believed to be the Bit Adini of the Assyrian inscriptions located on the Euphrates. The house of Eden or Beth Eden (Amos 1:5, see also 2 Chron. 29:12, 31:15). It is said that the melting of the snows in the Armenian mountains cause the river to overflow its bank each spring. Nebuchadnezzar is alleged to have controlled the floods by channeling and distributing the water throughout the whole country.

The quality of life for Adam and Eve after their expulsion from paradise was never the same until the day they died and returned to the dust of the ground. When it was proclaimed that the seed of the woman shall bruise the serpents head (Gen. 3:15). It was fulfilled at the cross through the seed of Abraham, Isaac, and Jacob by Christ our Savior" (Lk. 23:46). God's promise to Abraham was that his seed would inherit the land reaching the Euphrates (Gen. 15:18, Deut. 1:7, Josh. 1:4). Later, the Bible mentioned Eden was described as a delightful place (Isa. 51:3; Ezek. 28:13, 31:9, 16:18; and Joel 2:3). So of all the descriptions given in the Scripture of the delightful garden of Eden where the first family of God's creation once lived.

"Therefore, let the reader be aware of the Bible's account of Creation. (Genesis 1 and 2)—also proclaimed by the Psalmist: that declared thus."

"The heavens declare the glory of God, and the firmament sheweth his handywork. Day unto day uttereth speech, and night unto night sheweth knowledge. There is no speech nor language, where their voice is not heard" (Ps. 19:1–3). A statement of this fact has been proven and documented every day of our lives by the overwhelming evidence all around us. Apostle Paul writes, "For the invisible things of him from the creation of the world are clearly seen, being understood by the things that are made, even his eternal power and Godhead, so that they are without excuse" (Rom. 1:20). Notice Paul's use of the word *excuse*. Obviously, what this means is no one should be excused of his or her responsibility by justifying his or her unbelief, thereby refusing to accept the overwhelming evidence of God's creation without consequence. "The power of the Godhead are invisible things yet are clearly seen in their manifestation. He works in secret but manifests what he has wrought, making known his power known. The Godhead is known by the things they have made! These things did not make themselves. Therefore, an intelligent designer who could be no other than God the Creator of all that is good and pure must have made them.

Referring back to Adam and his sons and grandsons having this vast creation at his disposal, one would imagine that Adam did not spend his entire life in seclusion, wallowing in self-pity and eating herbs, grains, and vegetables. It is reasonable to assume he had some kind of hobby, like fishing in the great Euphrates with his sons and grandsons. A hobby he must have taught them. After all, some of Christ's disciples were fishermen.

A perfect illustration is the story of Peter's experience on the lake of Gennesaret. Peter, being a fisherman by trade, toiled all night and had taken nothing, at the command of Jesus, he was told to launch out into the deep and let down his net for a draught. Obediently, he did as he was instructed, "When they had this done, they enclosed a great multitude of fishes: and their net brake" (Lk. 5:6). In further study of these verses, we witness the result of being obedient to the divine will of God. However, by being disobedient, it has resulted in spiritual separation from the Lord, as in the case of Adam and Eve. Oh, what perfect fellowship Adam and his wife must have had with the Lord when they walked sinless together with the Lord in the garden of Eden. God communed with them in the cool of the day. However, the moment sin entered their lives, it separated them from the Lord so they hid themselves from his presence amongst the trees of the garden" (Gen. 3:8).

It is indescribable to think how it must have felt when Adam and his wife walked and communed with the Lord their Creator who has a plan of salvation before the foundation of the world you and me. Just think of how wonderful and effortless it must have been for our first parents before they fell from grace! Their only assigned work was to take care of the garden in accordance with the will of God without sweat or tears. But they failed, and life became very difficult for them when they had to toil and labor for their living. Because of their failure, however, the effect of their transgression has been felt throughout all generations.

Example of Peter's Failure and Reaction

The reaction of Peter's failure and disappointment when toiled all night fishing on the lake of Gennesaret and caught nothing. At first, his reaction was one of disappointment and frustration. However, when Jesus, being omniscient (all-knowing), told Peter to launch out into the deep and let down his net on the other side. Peter's obedience yielded him the largest catch of his fishing career (Lk. 5:1–11). This is a remarkable example of the only true God, the Creator who knows all things, even the needs of a disappointed fisherman.

In the preceding pages, I have discussed the cause and effect of Adam and Eve's transgressions and disobedience of the will of God. However, when one abides in the will of God, as in the example of Peter the fisherman, the result will be an eternal reward to the faithful. The biblical account of this true story shows Peter's initial reaction to Christs command to launch out into the deep water, a command that requires an act of obedience and trust despite our human effort to overcome life's daily struggle and the overwhelming odds against us. The example of Peter's willingness to obey teaches us that, the obedience to our Lord's command resulted in the reward of abundance of good that is, an abundant yield of fishes that it broke their net. When they called their partners, who were in another ship to come and help them, "they came, and filled both the ships, so that they began to sink" (Lk. 5:7). Peter's life was never the same since. Because of his obedience, however, Christ bestowed upon him, the title of "fishers of men" (Mk. 1: 17). As with his natural fishing expedition, he was not always successful in his spiritual evangelism either. Sometimes he experienced tremendous hostilities, including beatings and imprisonments; other times, even the very devil was subject to him. During those times when he was not so successful and suffered many disappointments, he was not deterred by his failures. Nevertheless, he went into even deeper waters and continued to fish for the hearts and souls of men and women everywhere. Although Peter's life was fraught with much danger, the end results brought forth a tremendous harvest of souls for the kingdom of heaven.

The story of Adam and Eve's rebellion and disobedience brought a much different result. Their acts of disobedience resulted in sin, pain, suffering, and death to the human race. Fortunately, Christ, the sacrificial Lamb slain from the foundation of the world, paid the price for Adam's fallen race (Lk. 23:46, Rev. 13:8). Going back to the beginning of Genesis, we see how the serpent tried to distort Gods truth with subtlety and clever distortion when he tempted the woman.

The serpent knew the exact command God gave to Adam and Eve, forbidding them to eat of the fruit of the tree in the midst of the garden, "God hath said, ye shall not eat of it neither shall ye touch it, lest ye die." Again, notice the distorted truth, "ye shall not surely die." Notice how the serpent continued to mix the truth with lies, when he said. "For God doth know that in the day ye eat thereof, then yours eyes shall be opened, and ye shall be as gods, knowing good and evil."(Gen. 3:5). Yes, their eyes were opened to sin for the first time. They were able to discern good from evil! Nevertheless, they did not become as gods, like the omniscient and omnipotent Creator described in Isaiah 40:18–25. "To whom will ye liken God? or what likeness will ye compare unto him?" (Isa. 40:18). "To whom then will ye liken me, or shall I be equal? saith the Holy One" (Isa. 40:25).

Although the above quotes deal in context with God's commitment to deliver the children of Israel from captivity and oppression, I believe it is well within the subject being discussed. To counter the serpent statement to the woman, implying that God was hiding the truth from them by saying if they would eat the forbidden fruit, their eyes would be open and they would become as gods" (Gen. 3:5). Although they did not die physically—the moment sin entered their lives, they did however, die spiritually. Hundreds of years later, they both experienced physical death for "when lust hath conceived, it bringeth forth sin: and sin, when it is finished, bringeth forth spiritual and physical death" (Jas. 1:15, emphasis added).

After days, weeks, months, and years went by and there was no immediate evidence of Adam and Eve's physical demise, perhaps in the eyes of the devil and the mindset of the natural person, the accuser might have said, "See, God could not be trusted when he told you that in the day that you eat of the forbidden fruit, you shall surely die." Because our first parents continued to live for a very long time after they had sinned, no doubt the devil must have thought he had won the victory over God and man.

However, not so fast, Lucifer! The God of all creation; the omnipotent, omniscient, all-knowing God has already made provision for the redemption of fallen man. Has Satan forgotten? Had he any realization or awareness of the fact that Christ was the Lamb slain from before the foundation of the world for the sins of fallen man? Do you remember what God told the serpent when the first trial in history of the human race was carried out in the garden of Eden? God cursed the serpent and condemn him to a life of creeping upon his belly and to eat the dust of the earth for the rest of his life; to the woman, he designated the task of childbearing with sorrows of labor pain; and to Adam, his sentence was commuted to a life of banishment from the garden of Eden to a life of toil and hard labor (Gen. 3:14–19).

No one knows for sure how Adam and Eve must have felt, living a life of guilt for such a long time as they have lived. Before man fell from grace, man and woman were made in the image of God to live and reign over every living creature of the earth forever. However, after Adam's death 930 years later and thereafter, "The days of our years are threescore years and ten; and if by reason of strength they be fourscore years" (Ps. 90:10).

2

THE FIRST BIRTH PAIN OF THE HUMAN RACE

The first human to experience pain and suffering was Eve, the first mother of the human race, experiencing labor pain in childbirth as the Lord said, "I will greatly multiply thy sorrow and thy conception; in sorrow, thou shalt bring forth children" (Gen. 3:16). This and all the other ills of society came about because of their transgression and disobedience.

Thousands of years later, James was inspired to write his epistle concerning the cause and effect of sin and transgression that reads:

> *Let no man say when he is tempted, I am tempted of God: for God cannot be tempted with evil, neither tempteth he any man, But every man is tempted, when he is drawn away of his own lust, and enticed. Then when lust hath conceived, it bringeth forth sin: and in, when it is finished, bringeth forth death. (Jas. 1:13)*

From that moment, when our first parents had transgressed, the process of deterioration of their once perfect bodies began to take place. No one can envision how Adam and Eve must have reacted when they first discovered their nakedness in the garden because of sin. Knowing they were created perfect in the image of God and had no need for anything except to fellowship with God their Creator, sin severed that unique fellowship they once enjoyed with their Creator. Although the serpent meant it for evil, God's divine plan of salvation made good come out of the controversy the enemy plotted against his will.

Now let us refer back to Genesis 1–3, there we can address the author's view more accurately. Let us say, for the sake of those who would like to refute the evidence of the Genesis account of the written word of God, when the serpent first deceived the woman, he probably thought that he won the victory over God and man. However, as time went by with no sign of Adam and Eve's physical demise, Satan must have said, "See, there was no truth to Gods command to you that in the day you eat of the fruit of the tree of the knowledge of good and evil, thou shalt surely die."

A great man once said, "Oh, what tangled web we weave when first we practice to deceive" (Sir Water Scott, "Marmion"). How true it is, judging from the result of sin throughout the history of mankind!

God's Timetable versus Prognosticators

In the fullness of time, God has always made good on his promises, no matter how long it takes. Just as God has declared to the woman that "he would greatly multiply her sorrow and her conception, in sorrows shall she bring forth children" (Gen. 3:16). Every woman, who has ever experienced natural childbirth can attest or bear witness to this stated fact. There are those, however, who do not believe anything the Bible has to say. Nevertheless, they cannot honestly deny the biblical fact that natural childbirth is indeed a painful experience from a woman's point of view. It is a medical and biological fact. The period between conception and normal childbirth is an average of 270 days with a range of about 250 to 310 days, approximately nine months. God, in his infinite wisdom, has determined it to be so in order for the embryo (fetus) in its earliest stage of life to develop into a viable living being.

In the foregoing statements, I have tried to be as concise as I could in my effort to point out the medical, biological, and scientific facts concerning the normal process of childbirth and its related complications. However, in the following examples, I will be more lucid in my presentation of facts from a biblical point of view. The views presented in the above statements are substantiated by medical and scientific facts. Is it not reasonable to accept a more irrefutable statement of fact from the representative of the all-knowing omnipotent Creator?

Take, for example, before God executes judgment upon a nation, he warns them through his prophets. Throughout the recorded history of the human race, men, women, and children have had the opportunity to escape the consequence of defiance to law and order in all phases of life, whether it is spiritual, secular, or physical. For example, if a child who was brought up to eat healthy and nutritious food conducive to healthy growth and carefully adhered to that lifestyle throughout his or her adulthood, chances are that person may experience less severe painful consequences in his or her lifetime. Though the consequences of healthy or unhealthy living may take a very long time to surface, it will have its intended effect. Likewise, this example is representative of those who abide in the will of God and adhere to his teachings. If we live right, we will receive a healthy and eternal reward.

Let us turn our attention to the word of God according to Isaiah the prophet. After a long time of suffering, God spoke to Isaiah to comfort his people with these words, "Before she travailed, she brought forth; before her pain came, she was delivered of a man child" (Isa. 66:7). Notice how God altered the natural laws of things to accomplish his divine will by bringing into being a nation without travail. Isaiah 66:8 described this observable fact and phenomena, "Who hath heard such a thing? who hath seen such things? Shall the earth be made to bring forth in one day? Shall a nation be born at once? for as soon as Zion travailed, she brought forth her children."

It is important for us to take notice and be aware of the fact that God alone is sovereign. Therefore, he does not need anyone's permission in order to alter the natural laws of things to intervene in the affairs of men according to his divine plan. As in the example of Zion and Jerusalem described in this text, Isaiah 66:10 explains, "Rejoice ye with Jerusalem, and be glad with her, all ye that love her: rejoice for joy with her, all ye that mourn for her." This should be of utmost concern to all believers that when one member of the body of Christ suffers, we all should express our concern, being partakers of the suffering of the body of Christ. Then the present sorrows shall soon be turned into abundance of joy to the faithful sufferers.

Divine Intervention

At this time, please allow me to elaborate on a few examples of God's divine intervention in the affairs of men by altering the natural laws of physics and nature on behalf of those he loves.

The parting of the Red Sea by God through his servant Moses, the commanding of the sun to standing still by his servant Joshua, and the parting of the Jordan River by Elijah and Elisha—all those noteworthy events in history clearly demonstrated the omnipotent power of a sovereign God, the Creator of heaven and earth and the universe.

Is there any among all the great men and women since the beginning of time who has ever laid claims to any of those extraordinary events in history? Certainly not Nimrod. "He was a mighty hunter before the Lord: wherefore it is said, Even as Nimrod the mighty hunter before the Lord. And the beginning of his kingdom was Babel" (Gen. 10:9–10). The great King Nebuchadnezzar of Babylon thought his kingdom would last forever until he came to his senses and his understanding returned to him (Dan". 4:29–34). Certainly not King Pharos of Egypt who held sway the children of Israel in bondage for over four hundred years until the Great I Am delivered them through his servant Moses. That was an extraordinary act of divine intervention in the affairs of men by the omnipotent God of all creation.

Great Men in History

History tells us that Alexander the Great tried to conquer the world in a short time and failed in his ambitious attempts. The king of Macedon (356-323 BC) had his son, Philip II, tutored by Aristotle. Upon succeeding to the throne in 336 BC, he won ascendancy over all of Greece by putting down uprisings in Thrace and Illyria and looked to Thebes. As head of an allied Greek army, he viewed himself as the champion of pan-Hellenism. He started East (334 BC) on what was to be the greatest conquest of ancient times. He defeated the Persians at the battles of Granicus (334 BC) and Issus. Tyre and Gaza fell after a year's struggle. He entered Egypt where he founded Alexandria. Moving to Mesopotamia, he overthrew the Persian Empire of Darius III at the battle of Gaugamela. Pushing on through eastern Persia, he invaded northern India, but there his forces would go no further. The fleet went back to the head of the Persian Gulf. Alexander himself led his soldiers through the desert, reaching Susa in. He died of fever a year later at age thirty-three. He was incontestably one of the greatest generals of all time and one of the most powerful personalities of antiquity.

Alexander the Great was, without question, a great conqueror of his time. However, his mortality demonstrated his fallibility, proving he was no match to the omnipotent God of all creation. This further illustrates the premise of my statements that only God can alter the laws of nature to bring forth the birth of a nation in a day without travail as depicted in Isaiah 66:7–9 in sharp contrast to Genesis 3:16.

The Awesomeness of the Creator

God is indeed an awesome God! "Who hath measured the waters in the hollows of his hand, and meted out heaven with the span, and comprehended the dust of the earth in a measure, and weighed the mountains in scales, and the hills in a balance?" (Isa. 40:12).

"All nations before him are as nothing; and they are counted to him less than nothing, and vanity. To whom then will you liken God? or what likeness will you compare unto him?" (Isa. 40:17–18).

The kings of Egypt and all the great kings and rulers of the earth—past, present, and future—are no match for the Great I Am. "I am Alpha and Omega, the beginning and the end, the first and the last" (Rev. 22:13).

In continuing with the subject of the awesomeness of the omnipotent God who is able to alter the laws of physics, science, nature, and gravity in whatever form may apply, the fact is there is no comparison to the Great I Am. You may judge for yourself by accepting or rejecting the words of his ambassador and representative Isaiah the prophet who declared, "All nations before him are as nothing, and they are counted to him less than nothing, and vanity. To whom then will you liken God? or what likeness will you compare unto him?" (Isa. 40:17–18). "To whom then will you liken me, or shall I be equal? Saith the Holy One Lift up your eyes on high, and behold who hath created these things" (Isa. 40:25–26).

It is important to note the significance of the question, To whom will you liken God or what likeness will you compare unto him? The answer is obvious! There is no comparison! Further explanation is given in my book, *From the Brink of Suicide*.

It is true that many great men in history have tried to imitate God to no avail. Lucifer has worked and is still working. He was defeated at the cross. Ultimately, his final death knell will soon be sounded.

Obviously, God has no equal. Whose report will you believe? As noted before, many of these questions are addressed in my book, *From the Brink of Suicide* by Simeon Johnson. Who can effectively argue his or her case against God? That would be a very painful experience. Many have tried, but history is full of their painful and disastrous end.

The Unparalleled Awesomeness of God

The awesome wonder and power of God is unparalleled. This reminds me of an experience my wife and I had on our vacation to Atlanta, Georgia, at our daughter's residence in the summer of July 1999. Our vacation experience was quite from the genuine hospitality shown by our daughter and her friends. We visited many historic sites, Dr. Martin Luther King childhood home and historic church. However, the highlight of my experience was a two-mile bus trip up to the top of a historic mountain, an experience I would categorize as very adventurous. I was inflamed with love and awe for the mountains as we ascended to the top! It captured my imagination and thoughts upon reaching the pinnacle of our assent. There I beheld the majestic display of the awesome wonder of God's creation.

While we were on the mountaintop, looking across the distant horizon and observing the burst of lightning and thunder, I began to imagine how Moses must have felt being alone with God on Mount Sinai while receiving the Ten Commandments. We are reminded by the writer of the book of Hebrews of the awesome display of the mountain "that burned with fire, nor unto blackness, and darkness, and tempest" (Heb. 12:18). It is beyond description to think of how an individual could witness the awesome display of God's awesome wonder—like a volcanic eruption, an earthquake, or any act of God for that matter—and dismiss it by saying, "Oh, it's just nature letting off steam!" "And the sound of a trumpet, and the voice of words: which voice they that heard intreated that the words should not be spoken to them any more" (Heb. 12:19). Anyone who has ever experienced the supernatural power of God, most assuredly would not be able to doubt it by asking, "Is it for real?" When Moses first saw the burning bush, if there were any doubts in his mind from a distance, as he got closer to God, all doubts vanished. Hebrews 12:21 reads, "And so terrible was the sight, that Moses said, I exceedingly fear and quake." Not a fear of doubt, however, but a fear of awe!

I am recapping the story of my vacation trip to Atlanta, Georgia, on a mountaintop experience that rejuvenated the memory of my experiences and relationship with the Lord. The incontestable awesomeness of God is incomparable. For those who say there is no God, I urge you to take a hike to the top of a mountain and imagine yourself in an earthquake with the magnitude of 8.5 on the Richter scale or higher. Can you see yourself shrugging it off—through divine intervention you were kept alive—by saying, "Oh, it's just nature letting off steam!" Most assuredly, you would not be so nonchalant in your thinking! Although I have never visited most of the nation's most magnificent mountains, I was spiritually and physically invigorated by the mountaintop experience of the awesome grandeur of God's magnificent creation. Admiring those majestic mountains, it's not hard to see the handiwork of the Creator for the entire world to see.

Rocky Mountains

Major mountain systems of North America form the continental divide and extend more than 3,000 miles (4,800 km) from New Mexico to Alaska. Mount Elbert, at 14,4431 feet (4,399 m), is the highest point of the Rocky Mountains. The mountains are topographically divided into the Southern, Central, and Northern Rockies (all in the U.S.), the Canadian Rockies, and the Brooks Range (Alaska). They are rich in minerals and lumber and are the sites of several national parks. These include Rocky Mountains, Yellowstone, Grand Teton, and Glacier national parks in the U.S. and Jasper, Banff, Glacier, Yoho, Kootenay, and Mount Revelstoke national parks in Canada. The Rockies were long a major barrier to transcontinental travel. The South Pass (Wyoming) is crossed by the Original Trail. However, the grandeur of those mountains are not there just for sightseers and curious onlookers, but to show the handiwork of God's creation.

The psalmist captured the essence of his word in this manner. "His lightnings enlightened the world: the earth saw and trembled. The hills melted like wax at the presence of the Lord, at the presence of the whole earth" (Ps. 97:4–5). This great majestic display of God's awesome wonder is clearly seen by all those who have eyes to see through all generations.

Lightning

The science of meteorology that deals with the atmosphere of a planet, particularly that of Earth, describes lightning as an electric discharge accompanied by thunder, commonly occurring during a thunderstorm. The release may take place between two parts of the same cloud, between two clouds, or between cloud and the earth. According to history, Benjamin Franklin proved the electrical nature of lighting in his famous kite experiment in 1752. Space probes have photographed lightning on Jupiter and recorded indications of it on Venus, Saturn, Uranus, and Neptune.

According to meteorological science, lightning occurs when a rain cloud will have a positively charged top and a negatively charged bottom. This negatively charged bottom induces a positive charge on the earth below it. When the interaction between the bottom of the cloud and the earth reaches a certain level, the air becomes ionized along a confined path, producing and discharge. The lightning acts like a discharge of a very large capacitor. The bottom of the clouds being one plate and the induced positive charge of the earth being the other. Arguably, there is still a lot of controversy over how the clouds become charge in the first place. Some say that ice must be present in the top of the clouds before they can become charged, and some say the opposite. Nevertheless, for the most part, lightning does seem to be attracted to metal or tall objects. There are personal accounts that contradict this theory, but one thing is for sure in our present understanding of lightning, it is practically impossible to predict with any degree of accuracy where it will strike.

However, according to the word of God in Jeremiah, "He hath made the earth by his power, he hath established the world by his wisdom, and hath stretched out the heavens by his discretion. When he uttereth his voice, there is a multitude of waters in the heavens, and he causeth the vapors to ascend from the ends of the earth; he maketh lightning with rain, and bringeth forth the wind out of his treasures" (Jer. 10:12–13). This, my friend, is the work of the omnipotent Creator of heaven and earth!

Appalachian Mountains

The Appalachian Mountains in one of the major North American mountain systems extending 1,600 miles (2,570 km) from Canada's Quebec province to Alabama with Mount Mitchell (2,037 m) in North Carolina as its highest point. The rugged hills and valleys, a severely eroded remnant of an ancient mountain mass, posed a significant barrier to westward expansion in the early years of U.S. industries include coal mining (in the West) and tourism.

Can anyone view the impressive, majestic sights of those mountains and after that decide to defy the natural laws of gravity by attempting to reach to their highest peak without proper preparations? Neither can they descend by leaping off their highest peaks without dire consequences.

We read in the scripture how that the devil tried to tempt our Lord to jump off the top of a high pinnacle by quoting the scripture and saying to him, "If thou be the Son of God, cast thyself down: for it is written, He shall give his angels charge concerning thee: and in their hands they shall bear thee up, lest at any time thou dash thy foot against a stone" (Matt. 4:6).

Yield Not to Temptation

Yielding to temptation is a sin! Christ did not yield to that or any other temptations from the devil. Instead, he responded with a candid rebuke. "It is written again. Thou shalt not tempt the Lord thy God" (Matt. 4:7). In that brief encounter, the devil should have known that Christ did not have to prove to him that he is the Son of God. Christ could have easily suspended gravity by stepping off any mountain. After all, he is the Creator of all things, both seen and unseen. Thankfully, he did not yield to the devil's temptations. "Thus saith the Lord, The heaven is my throne, and the earth is my footstool" (Isa. 66:1). It should be known to the devil and every one that the omnipotent one who is sovereign is able to do all that is in the perfect will of the Father! "For all those things hath my hand made, and all those things have been, saith the Lord" (Isa. 66:2).

The incontestable awesomeness of God is unparalleled. The devil should have known that his cheap offer of protection was not an offer too good to be refused. The psalmist quoted a prayer of Moses, a man of God. "Before the mountains were brought forth, or ever thou hadst formed the earth and the world, even from everlasting to everlasting, thou art God" (Ps. 90:2). Those are profound words of truth attributed to an awesome God, the God of all creation who made heaven and earth, including the mountains in all its grandeurs. The mountains have always been a place of great intrigue for many people, especially to those who have invested considerable interest in its mystique, like professional mountain climbers who have scaled many of their highest peaks.

Mountain Climbing

Mount Everest, at 8,846 m, is the highest mountain in the world. Located in the Himalayas on the Tibet-Nepal border. Named after Sir George Everest, the surveyor of the Himalayas, it was first climbed in 1953 by Sir Edmund Hillary and Tenzing Norkay after at least eight earlier attempts to scale it had failed. Along the eastern shore, there is a narrow continental shelf where high mountains rise abruptly from a sea floor. The Asian coast is low and fringed with islands rising from a wide continental shelf.

Mountain climbing is the practice of climbing to elevated points for sport, pleasure, or research. Also called mountaineering. The three principal types are: (1) trail climbing or hiking through forest trails to the top of small mountains; (2) rock climbing, the ascent of steeper mountains requiring the use of rope and steel spikes that are driven into the rock; and (3) ice climbing on very high mountains with peaks above the timber line. The golden age of mountain climbing began in the 1850s and ended with the conquest of the last of the great Alpine peaks, the Matterhorn in 1865.

I do believe, however, that the greatest fulfillment comes to those who aspire to experience the satisfaction of knowing that the Creator has been there before them and will be there with them, all the way to the top.

The Bible shows that many great men had their mountaintop experience with extraordinary results. Moses experienced the Lord on Mount Sinai; Elijah won the victory over the false prophets of Ba'al on Mount Carmel; and Peter, James, and John saw Jesus on the mount of transfiguration with Moses and Elias (Lk. 9:29–36). Christ and his disciples often retreated to the mountain to commune with the Father. Jesus had his Sermon on the Mount, commonly known as the Beatitudes. Jesus's triumphant ascension into heaven from Mount of Olive (Acts 1:10–12).

In our time, we had men like the late Dr. Martin Luther King who was widely known and honored for his commendable deeds in the civil rights movements. His "I Have a Dream" captured the hearts of the nation. The mountain and its awesome grandeur is a place of reflection, serenity, and humility of heart.

Lord of All, Including the Pacific Ocean

The Pacific Ocean is the world's largest ocean (181, 300,000 sq. km), occupying about one third of the Earth's surface between the West Coast of North and South America and the East Coast of Australia and Asia. It has a maximum length of c.9, 000 mi (14,500 km), a maximum width of c. 11, 000 mi (17,700 km), and a maximum depth of 36,198ft (11,033 m) in the Challenger Deep, In the Marinas Trench c.250 mi (400 km) SW of Guam. A series of volcanoes, the so-called Ring of Fire, encircles the ocean. Along the eastern shore, there is a narrow continental shelf and high mountains rise abruptly from a deep sea floor. The Asian coast is low and fringed with islands rising from a wide continental shelf.

But Christ is Lord of all! He is Lord over the mountains, over the great lakes and oceans. He has calmed the wind and the waves of the great lakes, when there arose a great tempest in the sea, "insomuch that the ship was covered with the waves, but he was asleep." And his disciples came to him, and awoke him, saying, "Lord, save us, we perish. And he said unto them, Why are you fearful, O ye of little faith? Then he arose, and rebuked the winds and the sea, and there was a great calm" (Matt. 8:24–26). Because there is no fear in him who has authority over the wind and the waves, therefore it was a simple thing for the Creator to rebuke the wind and the waves. His disciples to marveled, saying, "What manner of man is this, that even the winds and the sea obey him!" (Mt. 8:24). He could calm the wind and the waves of the mighty Pacific Ocean and walk safely on it just as easily.

Can any mortal do likewise? Certainly not! It is written. "Have you not known? have you not heard? hath it not been told you from the beginning? have you not understood from the foundations of the earth? It is he that sitteth upon the circle of the earth, and the inhabitants thereof are as grasshoppers; that stretcheth out the heavens as a curtain, and spreadeth them out as a tent to dwell in" (Isa. 40:21–22). Who in heaven or on earth can proclaim that, except the Creator of heaven and earth? No one else is able to do that! "All nations before him are as nothing, and they are counted to him less than nothing, and vanity" (Isa. 40:17).

The most brilliant minds that ever lived since time began, those who have left their mark and footprints on the sands of time, none can ever compare their achievement with the incomparable work of God's creation. Arguably, if man could chronologically compile a list of achievements of all the great men and women who left their mark in history, none could compare to the Creator of heaven and earth. God is an awesome God, so loving yet has shown his good humor through the psalmist, as you will notice in the following verses:

> *When Israel went out of Egypt, the house of Jacob from a people of strange language, Judah was his sanctuary, and Israel his dominion. The sea saw it, and fled: Jordan was driven back. The mountains skipped like rams and the little hills like lambs. What ailed thee, O thou sea, that thou wast driven back? Ye mountains that you skipped like rams, and ye little hills, like lambs? Tremble, thou earth, at the presence of the Lord, at the presence of the God of Jacob; Which turned the rock into standing waters, the flint into a fountain of waters.* (Ps. 114:1–8)

In psalm above, God revealed to his servant David, a man after God's own heart, that he is omnipotent, therefore, he alone can do the impossible. Can a man cause the mountain to skip like rams, the little hills like lambs? Has the sea ever fled before the presence of a man? Not ever! Although you may think of Moses parting the Red Sea, he could not have done it on his own accord! Only a sovereign God can do the impossible, including bringing to being the birth of a nation without travail (Isa. 66:7).

The Sovereignty of God

The sovereignty of God has been demonstrated by his supreme rule! "I am Alpha and Omega, the beginning and the ending, saith the Lord, and which was, and which is to come, the Almighty" (Rev. 1:8). The preeminence of his lordship is from everlasting to everlasting!

Realistically speaking, trying to define the sovereignty of God is more than mortal tongue can ever describe in words. Therefore, any attempt by man's finite ability in trying to fathom the mysteries of God is a futile attempt. He alone has spoken the world and the universe into existence and caused the sun, moon, stars, and all the planets to be in their proper orbit. He is able to alter the natural laws of gravity, allowing the sun to stand still, as he has done for Joshua (Josh. 10:12–14). Likewise, Moses parting the Red Sea and allowing the children of Israel to pass through on dry ground (Exod. 14:21). Four hundred years passed before the children of Israel were freed from the bondage of Egypt. God, who is sovereign, could have delivered them in one day, as depicted in Isaiah 66:7. God's ability to bring man to life, the birth of a man-child, to life or the birth of a nation in one day without travail or birth pain is not subject to the rule or control of another. Therefore, he does not have to negotiate or sign a peace treaty with anyone.

3
CREATION VERSUS MAN'S DECLARATION OF INDEPENDENCE FROM HIS CREATOR

The authentic words of the declaration of Creation declare emphatically:

In the beginning God created the heaven and the earth. And the earth was without form, and void; and darkness was upon the face of the deep. And the Spirit of God moved upon the face of the waters. And God said, Let there be light: and there was light. And God saw the light, that it was good: and God divided the light from the darkness. (Gen. 1:1–4)

Other inspired writers of the declaration of creation testify to the authenticity of creation. "The heavens declare the glory of God; and the firmament showeth his handywork. Day unto day uttereth speech, and night unto night sheweth knowledge. There is no speech nor language, where voice is not heard" (Ps. 19:1–3).

The awesome wonder of God's creation is incomprehensible, therefore the natural mind is incapable of comprehending the wisdom and knowledge of the omniscient, all-knowing Creator of heaven and earth. "For the invisible things of him from the creation of the world are clearly seen, being understood by the things that are made, even his eternal power and Godhead, so that they are without excuse" (Rom. 1:20).

Testimonials

The culminating testimonials of the declaration of creation are highlighted in:

> *In the beginning was the word, and the Word was with God. The same was in the beginning with God. All things were made by him; and without him was not anything made that was made. In him was the life; and the life was the light of men. And the light shineth in darkness; and the darkness comprehended it not. (Jn. 1:.l–5)*

Are there not overwhelming evidence presented in these stated facts? For those who are not convinced of the facts presented, let us reason together without looking aimlessly for the truth. Here, our road map directs us to our spiritual blueprint found in 1 John, which reads as follows:

> *That which was from the beginning, which we have heard, which we have seen with our eyes, which we have looked upon, and our hands have handled, of the Word of life, (For the life was manifested, and we have seen it, and bear witness, and show unto you that eternal life, which was with the Father, and was manifested unto us;) That which we have seen and heard declare we unto you, that ye also may fellowship with us: and truly our fellowship with the Father, and with his Son Jesus Christ. And these things write we unto you, that your joy may be full. This then is the message, which we have heard of him, and declare unto you, that God is, light, and in him is no darkness at all" (1 Jn. 1:1–5)*

David the psalmist, a man after Gods own heart, declared, "Lord, thou hast been our dwelling place in all generations. Before the mountains were brought forth, or ever thou hadst formed the earth and the world, even from everlasting to everlasting, thou art God" (Ps. 90:1–2). Who would want to refute such a powerful testimony?

Jesus, the Son of God, testified of his creation. "Verily, verily, I say unto thee, We speak that we do know, and testify that we have seen; and ye receive not our witness. If I have told you earthly things, and ye believe not, how shall ye believe, if I tell you of heavenly things? (Jn. 3:11–12). Jesus later affirmed that among the men who were born of a woman, there is none greater than John the Baptist. "And what he hath seen and heard, that he testifieth; and no man receiveth his testimony. He that hath received his testimony hath set to the seal that God is true" (Jn. 3: 32–33).

These testimonies are also confirmed in John 1:1–5 who spoke of his beginning with complete assurance and certitude regarding his character, ability, and strength. John also testified in his epistle His eyewitness account of him who made all things.

Solomon, the wisest man who ever lived, was inspired to write of his existence. "The Lord possessed me in the beginning of his way, before his works of old. I was set up from everlasting, from the beginning, or ever the earth was" (Prov. 8:22–23).

Mr. Darwin, were you there? Using your God-given knowledge, conducting research in order to discredit your Creator? If so, tell us when and where Mr. Darwin? The world would like to see and know the evidence of your thesis. Could you honestly attribute these claims to your findings? Can you make the following claims:

"When he appointed the foundations of the earth: Then I was by him, as one brought up with him: and I was daily his delight, rejoicing always before him; rejoicing in the habitable part of his earth; and my delight were with the sons of men" (Prov. 8:29–31)?

SIMEON W. JOHNSON

The Declaration God's Creation Is Unparalleled

We know God's Creation is unparalleled from the evidence presented and the five senses God gave us. However, for the sake of those who would argue on behalf of the physically disabled or lost any of their five senses, these God-given gifts from birth are universal.

The five senses given to us from birth:

- *Seeing.* What we perceive by the eye. The heavens declare the creation of God with its innumerable constellation of stars in our galaxy and beyond our known universe. It is impossible for anyone to count the number of stars in the heavens, except the Creator himself! Only the omnipotent, omniscient, and superior intelligence God could create the world and the universe with all its infinite number of stars, such magnificent celestial splendor unfathomable to our finite minds.

- *Hearing.* The process or power of perceiving sound. "Day unto day uttereth speech, and night unto night sheweth knowledge. There is no speech nor language, where their voice is not heard" (Ps. 19:2–3). We hear the sound of the wind, but we cannot tell where it is coming from and where it is going. Nevertheless, can we deny its existence just because we hear the sound but cannot see it?

- *Feeling.* The power to respond or an act of responding to stimuli; the power to touch: From the moment a child is born, if the birth is normal, then the sense of is essential. Henceforth, the maternal bond between mother and child begins and ends only in death!

- *Tasting.* To try or determine the flavor of something: Our first mother and father could not resist the desire of tasting the forbidden fruit!

- *Smelling.* To perceive the odor of using something special senses. We smell the sweet fragrance of the beautiful flowers as they bloom at springtime! The pleasant aroma of your wife or love one's perfume! Isn't it sweet and lovely, good and pleasant to be able to smell the fragrance of your loved one and the things we love?

All these good gifts and blessings that the Creator has given us through our five senses, should they not be able to convince us of an intelligent Creator who made all these things possible? Man, on the other hand, has been declaring his independence from his Creator since ancient time. Then came Charles Darwin in 1859 with his doctrine of the theory of evolution, which continues to this day. The eternal Great I Am is—and always is—God! This makes the argument of Darwin's theory of evolution null and void. The word of God and the overwhelming supporting evidence of Creation espouse this fact!

Creation is not just a random act of matter smashing into each other as the scientists would have us believe, despite the facts and all that has been proven and demonstrated. Whose credibility will you trust, man's flawed credibility or Gods impeccable credibility? After careful evaluation of the overwhelming evidence of Creation, please choose the biblical account, not men's. Therefore, "let God be true, but every man a liar" (Rom. 3:4).

Alleged Human Evolution

The theory of human evolution alleges that the human species, Homo sapiens, and their immediate ancestors known as hominids (notable for being bipedal) through a low rate of maturation and large brains developed relatively sophisticated capacity for language, tool use, and social activity. About five million years ago, human and apes began to develop along separate lines. The earliest known hominid fossil is of the genus Australopithecus (about 4.4 million years ago), allegedly so. It does not hurt however, if they would try sticking to the facts for a change. That is the word and the overwhelming evidence of the Creator's handiwork.

Let us turn to the authentic word of the Creator who was there from the beginning. "Gird up now thy lion like a man, for I demand of thee, and answer thou me. Where was thou when I laid the foundations of the earth? declare, if thou hast understanding. Who has laid the measures thereof, if thou knowest? or who hath stretched the line upon it?" (Job 38:3–5). Obviously, the answer to the questions is clear to the believers. But for those who do not believe, to whom do you attribute the premise of the question and answer? It cannot be to Darwin's theory of evolution.

One cannot help but be filled with sorrow and dismay how men with such astute knowledge and intelligence, like anthropologists, archaeologist, and geologist, who have gone to the ends of the earth to search for evidence of Creation when the evidence is right there in front of you! Right where you stand! The word of God according to 2 Thessalonians 2:11 said, "God shall send them strong delusion, that they should believe a lie:" What could be further from the truth than for a person to say, "There is no God" and that man is only a product of natural selection through the process of evolution. Man has declared his independence from his Lord by denying the deity and lordship of the Creator, thereby severing all ties and relationship with his Maker by endorsing the big bang theory of how the world and the universe came into existence. We will be discussing some of the issues at hand next.

The Origins of Man According to Evolution

Scientists piece together man's family tree one branch at a time. They dig out primitive tools, and bones at an Ethiopian site. The painstaking work requires patience and dedication family tree.

See how the creature might fit in. Lucy: An older sister or distant relation…

In Genesis, God made the earth! "And the earth brought forth grass and herb yielding seed after his kind, and the tree yielding fruit, whose seed was in itself, after his kind: and God saw that it was good"

(Gen. 1:12). Therefore, there is no need for man to mess things up by throwing a monkey wrench into God's finished creation with an unproven theory of evolution.

Ardipithecus Ramidus

The most primitive hominid found in 1974, this species has more features of a chimpanzee than any other human ancestor does. Allegedly, the Ardipithecus ramidus might have walked upright. Other fossils discovered suggest that the species lived in the forest 4.4 million years ago. How can one who is finite equate time to him who is *eternal*, with no beginning and no ending?

"When he gave to the sea his decree, that the waters should not pass his commandment: when he appointed the foundations of the earth: Then I was by him, as one brought up with him: and I was daily his delight, rejoicing always before him; Rejoicing in the habitable part of the earth; and my delight were with the sons of men" (Prov. 8:29–31). His angels, he created as messengers and ministering servants of God, rejoiced in his creation when he appointed the foundations of the earth long before Darwin arrived on planet Earth.

We are here on this earth by the divine will of God, the offspring of man and woman who were made in the image of God our Creator, not by natural selection from primitive species of apes and chimpanzees. The Lord said, "Behold, I have graven thee upon the palm of my hands" (Isa. 49:16). Therefore, whose report will you believe, man's flawed report or the profound declaration of the infallible word of God? Let us hear what Isaiah has to say concerning the knowledge of his name from his mother's womb! "Listen, O isles, unto me; and hearken, ye people, from far; The Lord hath called me from the womb; from the bowels of my mother hath he made mention of my name" (Isa. 49:1).

To which of the hominid species of the animal kingdom has God communicated this intimate knowledge? Are there any offspring of primitive apes and chimpanzees capable of logic reasoning to think and ponder over such profound statements? The answer is a resounding no!

SIMEON W. JOHNSON

Probability versus Wishful Thinking

To which of the animal kingdom or inanimate object has the Creator ever pronounced such declaration of future events that has come to pass exactly as foretold? The seed of the woman shall bruise the serpents head, and it shall bruise his heel. This happened exactly as foretold in Genesis 3:15 at Calvary (Lk. 23:46): The probability of that prediction between ever happening to animals is impossible.

The evolutionist may not agree with such stated fact despite the overwhelming supporting evidence of the Genesis account of Creation. For example, here are some indisputable proof. "The wind blows where it listeth, and thou hearest the sound thereof, but canst not tell whence it cometh, and whither it goeth" (Jn. 3:8). Can anyone deny the effect and sound of the wind? That can happen only if you are not truly honest with yourself. So to my evolutionist readers and all Bible-believing mothers, fathers, and grandparents. When your children and grandchildren come home from school or various institutions of higher learning and confronts you with questions about Darwin's theory of evolution, a philosophy that is regrettably quite popular in our culture today, just inform them that God taught Adam that God created the heaven and the earth; the sun, moon, and stars; and the universe.

Adam and Eve became the first teachers of the human race. Teach your children and grandchildren the following verses: "In the beginning God created the heaven and the earth" (Gen. 1:1). He saw that it was good and said, "Let us make man in our own image" (Gen. 1:26). "In the image of God created he him; male and female created he them" (Gen. 1:27) and "breathed into his nostrils the breath of life; and man became a living soul" (Gen. 2:7). Of body, soul, and spirit throughout the Scriptures, these are the facts that need to be taught to our children and grandchildren—there is no other God who can deliver after this sort.

The Consequence of Rebellion

Did the children and grandchildren of Adam and Eve adhere to their teachings? Except for Able, Enoch, and Noah. as far as we know, there is little that we know of the others who may or may not have followed the teachings of Adam and Eve, the first family during the Antediluvian age.

Starting from chapter six of the book of Genesis, we begin to see the evidence of the history of relativism evolving into a dangerous idea of atheism, agnosticism, and, perhaps even the atheistic idea of evolution. If there is any doubt in the validity of the said statements? All one has to do is to verify these statement in reference to chapters 6 and 7 of Genesis. If the men, women, and children of that generation followed the teachings of God, they would not have come to that conclusion that there is no God for man to trust and obey. Therefore, they took upon themselves to sin with impunity.

Notice what God said in Genesis 6:1, which reads, "And it came to pass, when men began to multiply on the face of the earth, and daughters were born unto them." Take note of the phrase, "were born unto them." This clearly referred to the union between men and women, not with members of the same sex. Confirming the Bible's account of Creation, not by random selection of the species through natural selection or survival of the fittest through the process of evolution.

The Triumph of Good over Evil

"And God saw the wickedness of man was great in the earth, and that every imagination of the thoughts of his heart was only evil continually" (Gen. 6:5). This clearly indicates that man's heart was so wicked that every imagination and desire of his heart was to do evil continually. That is why the prophet Jeremiah was inspired to write words to the same effect in Jeremiah 17:9.

Despite man's rebellion, however, *Jehovah-jireh* (God will provide) has his plan of salvation to redeem those he foreknew and predestinated.

This has been demonstrated in the rapture of Enoch, before the great flood came and destroyed them all except Noah, his wife, his three sons, and their wives. Only eight souls were saved in the ark on that great flood (Genesis 7:13). Oh, what marvelous extension of grace and love our Creator has toward fallen man. He could have destroyed the entire human race by a global flood, but he did not. Thank God! Instead of destroying the human race, he has kept his promises made to the woman in Genesis 3:15. This extension of grace and love through his divine plan of salvation was fulfilled during the great flood that almost destroyed the human race. Unfortunately, Satan thought he nailed Christ to the cross, bruising the heel of the seed of the woman. However, Christ's triumphant resurrection from the dead, bruising the serpent's head as declared in the Scripture. That is an undeniable fact, an argument the evolutionist simply cannot win.

Metamorphism

According to geologists, the natural process of change in the structure and composition of rocks are caused by heat, deforming pressure, and/or chemically active fluids. In general, metamorphic rocks are coarser, denser, and less porous than the rock from which it was formed. The change in texture commonly results in a rearrangement of mineral particles into a parallel alignment called foliation, probably the most characteristic property of metamorphic rocks. It is seen in *slate*, *schist*, and *gneiss*. Local metamorphism is usually caused by the intrusion of a mass of igneous rock into older rock. Regional metamorphism accompanies mountain-building activity associated with large-scale crustal movements.

It is not difficult to imagine how such conclusion gave credence to the formation of man's opinion of Creation, choosing rather to believe the false doctrine of the big bang theory of evolution and denying the declaration of creation, according to the Genesis account. We continue with the subject of man's decision to sever ties with his Creator, declaring his independence from the sovereignty of his Lord. "And God saw the wickedness of man was great in the earth, and that every imagination of the thoughts of his heart was only evil continually" (Gen. 6:5). As it is written, "Where sin abounded, grace did much more abound" (Rom. 5:20).

Let us take for example the prefect atonement for sin. What can wash away our sins? Nothing but the blood of Jesus! "For the life of the flesh is in the blood: and I have given it to you upon the altar to make an atonement for your soul: for it is the blood that maketh an atonement for the soul" (Lev 17:11). Therefore, there is no other God who could make this possible except the eternal Creator himself!

4

THE BEST CURE FOR AIDS

Disease caused by strains of a virus known as human immunodeficency virus (HIV) that attacks certain white blood cells called T cells or CD4. According to medical science, the virus is spread through the exchange of body fluids—primarily semen, blood, and other fluids—and can persist in the body for a decade or more without any apparent symptoms.

Drug used to treat patients infected with HIV, which cause AIDS, also called azidothymidine, inhibits the virus's ability to reproduce and may decrease the frequency of infection by other diseases, enhancing the lives of HIV-infected patients but does not cure AIDS. Two other drugs that act similar to AZT, didanosine (DDI) or dideoxyinosine and stavudine (d4T) are used to treat patients who do not respond to or cannot tolerate AZT. Another similar acting drug, zalcitabine (ddC) or dideoxycytidine] is given in combination with AZT.

The disease weakens the body's immune system, allowing other diseases, including Kaposi's sarcoma (KS), an otherwise relatively uncommon and benign form of cancer; Pneumocystis carinii pneumonia (PCP); pulmonary tuberculosis; invasive cervical cancer; and encephalitis to overwhelm the individual. Very frightening! This is scary stuff! Nevertheless, there is hope that transcends all that scary stuff. Would you like to hear about it?

Allow me to recommend you to the best cure for the AIDS and all that ails you! In all fairness and honesty, the solution to your problems is the perfect blood transfusion, the *blood atonement*.

Divine Atonement

This divine atonement can be traced right back to the garden of Eden when Adam and Eve's sin separated them from their Creator who created man in his own image and breathed into him the breath of life. Then man became a living soul with body and spirit. Because of sin and disobedience, however, the only thing that could atone and redeem man back to God, his Creator, is blood sacrifice of divine acceptance. Further evidence of this fact has been demonstrated when the blood sacrifice of Abel, Adam's first son, was accepted unto God, but the sacrifice of Cain was rejected because it was not a blood sacrifice unto God his Creator!

God continues to demonstrate his love toward us as Christ, our Redeemer, was made the sacrificial Lamb as "the only begotten of the Father, full of grace and truth" (Jn. 1:14). "The Lamb of God, slain from the foundation of the world" (Rev. 13:8). "The blood of sprinkling, that speaketh better things than that of Abel" (Heb. 12:24) has shed his precious blood on the cross for our sins so that men and women of Adam's fallen race can be redeemed back into his favor again. Oh, what marvelous plan and act of redeeming love the Father has demonstrated to redeem fallen man. Only Jehovah-jireh, our Creator and provider, can deliver us, not an inanimate fossil rock or mere mortal with finite limitations. Is there any other like the omnipotent, omniscient, and all-knowing God who could have made man from the dust of the ground into a living being with a soul, body, and spirit? There is no other god, no art and science based on the theory of evolution can create flesh and blood out of the dust of the ground like the Creator has done!

Let us continue with the discussion of the unique life through blood atonement! By means of cloning or artificial insemination, who will ever produce a near perfect species in the form of a human being then breathe life into what he made as flesh and blood? The answer to the question is a resounding no! Let the word of God stand sure; that is, with God, there is no equal. Neither is there any likeness unto him. Therefore, any attempt to imitate or duplicate any act of God's creation, one would have to be able to make something out of nothing. Only the true and living God can create something out of nothing. By this may all men know! Only the perfect blood of the Lamb of God can truly atone for the sins of man, and that is the fact that wins every contest!

Food for Thought

This is a redacted chapter of my first book. We are living in a very fearful time in history where everyone is afraid of the dreaded disease called AIDS. To the layperson who is not extensively trained in the physiology of the human body, one might ask why the disease be transmitted through the bloodstream. This is what the Bible has to say about it! We read in Leviticus 17:11, "For the life of the flesh is in the blood: and I have given it to you upon the altar to make atonement for your souls: for it is the blood that maketh atonement for the soul."

That's right, the life is in the blood. Therefore, if the blood is contaminated, it will eventually destroy the whole body. For the said reasons, who in his or her right mind would want to mingle with contaminated blood? Think of one person in this world who is dearest to you. No doubt the majority of people would say their mother or their wife or whomever. Because of the fear of AIDS in the world today, no one wants to be given a questionable transfusion or mingle with contaminated blood. Not even if you were aware that that contaminated blood is the blood of your dearest love one. However, there is one person whose blood not only mingles with my blood and whose blood I'm not afraid of catching AIDS from because it has cleansed me and made me whole! The precious blood is none other than that of our Lord Jesus Christ. In order to save us from the impending judgment of God, wash us with the blood to save us, and not kill us with AIDS. According to Romans 5:9, "Much more then, being now justified by his blood, we shall be saved from wrath through him." In Ephesians 1:7, we read, "In whom we have redemption through his blood, the forgiveness of sins, according to the riches of his grace." The blood of Jesus is perfect in grace and mercy for the atonement of sin. Apostle Paul reiterates the same proclamation concerning the redemptive power of the blood of Jesus as declared above. Colossians 1:14 reads, "In whom we have redemption through his blood, even the forgiveness of sins," summing up the subject of the blood of Jesus and its redemptive power to forgive sins.

Let us now focus on the need for confessing our sins to Jesus from his cleansing blood that atones for our sins. "But if we walk in the light, as he is in the light, we have fellowship one with another, and the blood of Jesus Christ his Son cleanseth us from all sin. If we say that we have no sin, we deceive ourselves, and the truth is not in us. If we confess our sins, he is faithful and just to forgive us of all sins, and to cleanse us from all unrighteousness. If we say that we have not sinned, we make him a liar, and his word is not in us" (1 Jn. 1:7–10). Praise the Lord!

There you have it! The infallible word of truth, proclaiming the blood of Jesus to be the only blood that can save souls! There is no fear in this blood. The only fear is found in those who refused to accept its cleansing power to forgive sins. *A soul is a precious thing to waste!*

5

HE LOVES US LIKE NO OTHER

*For whom the Lord loveth he chastenth, and
scourgeth every son whom he receiveth.*
—Hebrews 12:6

Let me begin this frame of reference, pertaining to the subject matter of. The writer has given us an in-depth illustration of what chastening is all about. One of the many illustrations given states, "Now no chastening for the present seems to be joyous, but grievous: nevertheless, afterward it yieldeth the peaceable fruit of righteousness unto them which are exercised thereby" (Heb. 12:11). This is a profound statement of fact.

Have you ever experienced a time in your life where the trials of life seems so overwhelmingly unbearable? At such moment, how you wish you had wings like a dove to fly away and be at rest. Many people indeed express this sentiment. I'm quite sure many would share the same prevailing view. Nonetheless, for those of us who are enthusiastic animal lovers, doesn't it peak our interest to a certain degree?

As we observe the animal kingdom, especially our domesticated pets, they instinctively enjoy their freedom, unlike that of us human beings. Let's take the birds, for example, how they soar and glide gracefully through the air. The cats purr and frolic contentedly as they walk softly to and fro, softer than the sound of the lowest decibel frequency that the human ears can audibly detect. They live their lives as though they have not a care in the world! I do realize, however, that even man's best friends do suffer cognitive disorder and separation anxiety from time to time. When their owners have to take them to the animal shelters to go away on a vacation, their veterinarians normally recommend Anipryl and Prozac to treat their pets' depression from anxiety disorder. With the exception of those pets that do experience this sort of disorder, their overall life is one of freedom and without a care in the world!

By contrast, for the most part, most humans do not spend their time like the birds, cats, dogs, or other domesticated animals! Nevertheless, we do have a better future that speaks of better things than that of our animal friends. The truth is, "If in this life only we have hope in Christ, we are of all men most miserable" (1 Cor. 15:19). Therefore. in the final analysis of the subject matter, one need not look very far to find a special person without a unique experience of suffering of one kind or the other. Every human being who ever lived and walked on the face of this earth has, at some point in time, experience sufferings in his life in one way or the other.

A unique example we might consider at this time is the patriarch Enoch. Although we do not know much of the life and sufferings of Enoch, we do know from the scripture, "All the days of Enoch were three hundred and sixty five years" (Gen. 5:23). During those years of his life, he must have at least endured temptation and persecution, through the devises of the devil, from his peers and enemies. Friends and foes alike! A perfect example is seen in Jesus who was tempted by the devil yet he did not sin. The scripture said, "And Enoch walked with God: and he was not: for God took him" (Gen. 5:24). Nevertheless, a prophetic inspiration was revealed to Jude, a man of God.

> *And Enoch also, the seventh from Adam, prophesied of these, saying, Behold, the Lord cometh with ten thousands of his saints. To execute judgment upon all, and to convince all that are ungodly among them of their ungodly deeds which they have ungodly committed, and all their hard speeches which ungodly sinners have spoken against him. These are*

> *murmurers, complainers, walking after their own lusts; and their mouth speaketh great swelling words, having men's persons in admiration because of advantage. (Jude 1:14–16)*

Again, if Enoch had not known persecution and suffering, he would not have prophesied thus!

Perfect Love that Chastens

"For what glory is it, if when ye be buffeted for your faults, ye shall take it patiently? but if, when ye do well, and suffer for it, ye take it patiently, this is acceptable with God" (1 Pet. 2:20). Let's take, for example, a biblical personality in the person of David, a man after God's own heart. A real life story that is synonymous with chastening and suffering in the lives of believers whom he has called unto his own and is reflective of all believers. I would like to emphasize two essential points before I proceed with the story of David's rise and fall, depicting man's weaknesses.

The children of Israel were a peculiar people chosen to be different from all the families of the earth (Amos 3:2). However, they rebelled against God and his appointed leaders and chose to have a king to reign over them like all the other nations (1 Sam. 8:5–6). Despite Samuel's pleas and admonitions to them about the advantages and disadvantages of choosing their own king, they vehemently rejected his pleas. "And the Lord said unto Samuel, Hearken unto the voice of the people in all that they say unto thee: for they have not rejected thee, but they have rejected me, that I should not reign over them" (1 Sam. 8:7).

The story continues as we see the results of disobedience and rebellion when a person or nation rejects God and takes matters into their own hands. The end results inevitably lead to chaos, confusion, and ultimate destruction.

A King Not Chosen by Divine Will

Saul, their chosen king was ultimately rejected by the Lord as a result of disobedience and rebellion. First Samuel 13:14 reads, "But now thy kingdom shall not continue: the Lord hath sought him a man after his own heart, and the Lord hath commanded him to be captain over his people, because thou hast not kept that which the Lord commanded thee." This is a solemn warning to all who walk contrary to the will of God and choose to do things their own way.

After Saul's death, the drama in David's life begins to unfold. God's plan of salvation continued since the creation of Adam and Eve, our first parents. Saul, rejected by God, began the process of anointing the chosen king of Israel who would ultimately produce the seed proclaimed by God to the woman in Genesis 3:15. This seed is the lineage the Messiah would come from.

A Chosen King

David, a man after God's own heart, his rise and fall is illustrated in 1 Samuel 16:1. Time and space do not permit me to write in detail every chapter, every verse, and every line of all that transpired in the saga of David's life. However, I will try to highlight the essential points of the story as I endeavor to be led by the Spirit and inspiration of the word of God.

The story begins thus, "And the Lord said unto Samuel, How long wilt thou mourn for Saul, seeing I have rejected him from reigning over Israel? fill thine horn with oil, and go, I will send thee to Jesse the Bethlehemite: for I have provided me a king among his sons" (1 Sam. 16:1).

God's Will for Our Lives

God's will for our lives requires each of us to obey his command, to go where he wants us to go, to do what he tells us to do, and to follow his instructions. When God told Samuel to go and make a sacrifice, Samuel said, "How can I go? If Saul hear it, he will kill me. And the Lord said, Take an heifer with thee, and say, I am come to sacrifice to the Lord" (1 Sam. 16:2). God told Samuel to call Jesse to the sacrifice. "And thou shalt anoint unto me him whom I name unto thee" (1 Sam.16:3). The process of salvation progresses. Samuel did what the Lord told him to do upon his arrival at Bethlehem. We've seen an example of man's carnality from man's point of view, but as we look through the unseen eyes of the omniscient, all-knowing God, we see a different picture. "But the Lord said unto Samuel, look not on his countenance, or the height of his stature; because I have refused him: for the Lord seeth not as man seeth; for man looketh on the outward appearance, but God looketh on the heart" (1 Sam. 1:7). The rest of the sons of Jesse were rejected (verses 8–11). Verse 11 gives us an interesting example of God's wonder working power that no other power can do. When Samuel asked Jesse if there were any other children, "And he said, There remaineth yet the youngest, and, behold, he keepeth the sheep" (1 Sam. 16:11). Note the key words here, "and, behold, he keepeth sheep." A perfect reminder of how God can use the base things like the dust of the ground to create man in his own image and out of that dust of ground, "the process of man's redemption is completed" (Jn. 19:30).

Before we get to the end, however, let's remind ourselves that before the finished work, there was a beginning! Henceforth, the story of the redemption process continues. The scripture said, "But God has chosen the foolish things of the world to confound the wise; and God hath chosen the weak things of the world to confound the things which are mighty" (1 Cor. 1:27).

Being Chastened for a Purpose

"Now no chastening for the present seemeth to be joyous however, but grievous: nevertheless it yieldeth the peaceable fruits of righteousness unto them which are exercised by it" (Heb. 12:11). How does this correlate with the evidence of creation, you may ask. From the origin of all life form as stated in Genesis chapters 1–3 and continues throughout the genealogy of the human race.

The word of God is final. God is the author and finisher of our faith, therefore trust in God's word, not the words of finite man. We are not the product and offspring of humanoids or apes, neither have we evolved as a result of selective mutation as the evolutionist alleged. We are human beings made in the image of God our Creator!

What college or university have you graduated from that qualifies you to make the statements you are making? The answer is the "university" of the Word of God. Jesus, the author and finisher of my faith, of which I am a humble student of the word of the only true wise God (see Acts 4:13). "The fear of the Lord is the beginning of wisdom" (Prov. 9:10), therefore no power on earth—colleges, universities, or institutions of higher learning—can outsmart the wisdom of the Most High God.

Getting back to the subject of David, God's chosen king of Israel. Notice that after all the other sons were rejected, we see the choice is now fit and ready to be the anointed king of Israel. "And he sent, and brought him in. Now he was ruddy, and withal [having handsome eyes] of beautiful countenance, and goodly to look to. And the Lord said, Arise, anoint him: for this is he" (1 Sam. 16:12, emphasis mine).

Will versus Desire

We have learned from the story of David's life that God's plan of redemption for Adam's fallen race has always been right on target, not a moment too soon. Nevertheless, knowing the imperfect nature of mankind, somewhere along the way, we are always getting in the way of God's good and perfect will for our lives.

Case in point, not long after he was anointed king, we read in 1 Samuel 16:13 that the Spirit of the Lord came upon David. From that day forward, as long as he was in the will of God his Creator and the favor of the Lord was with him, he became Saul's armourbearer (1 Sam. 16:21).

On the other hand, when sin and pride gets into the hearts of men, it's always a recipe for disaster. In David's victory over Goliath, one of the greatest stories of the Bible, notice the accolade given to David, "And the women answered one another as they played, and said, Saul hath slain his thousands, and David his ten thousands" (1 Sam. 18:7). Saul was very angry with the praise given to David, henceforth displeasure manifested into venomous hatred. "And Saul eyed David from that day and forward" (1 Sam. 18:9). Such bitter hatred led the way to David's struggle with chastening by his enemies throughout his forty-year reign as king of Israel.

6

THE BATTLE OF THE WILL VERSUS THE CHASTENING OF THE ENEMY

During the forty-year reign of King David, he spent much of his life hiding from Saul in dens and caves throughout the land of Israel. Once he committed that grievous sin with Bathsheba, the wife of Uriah, his most trusted and loyal solder. Not only did he commit adultery with her, he also had Uriah killed by sending him at the frontline in the heat of battle. The plot thickened when he tried to cover it up. That, however, did not please the Lord. Henceforth, his struggle escalated to the point of falling into the hands of an angry God. Allow me at this time to interject an earlier quote. "Oh, what tangled web we weave, when first we practice to deceive!" (Sir Walter Scott).

It is written, "But where sin abounded, grace did much more abound" (Rom. 5:20). The sovereign Lord is always willing and able to show mercy according to his good and perfect will and purpose. Ever since the beginning of time, however, Satan is always trying to thwart and subvert God's plan of salvation. He has never succeeded and never will! The Lord made a promise that from the lineage of David would come forth the Messiah. Henceforth, the evidence of Creation and the promise made to the woman in Genesis 3:15 has been preserved and fulfilled by Christ's birth, death, burial, and resurrection. Can the doctrine of Darwin's theory of evolution in the 1800s live up to the kind of scrutiny as the Bible has and withstand the test of time since the beginning? Certainly not!

Declared Statements of Facts

"There is no speech nor language where their voice is not heard!" I am a living witness to this stated fact. Over thirty-five years ago at the age of seventeen, I was living a life of hopelessness, despair, and partial indifference and running away from God, sometimes not being mindful at all.

Does anyone think they can hide away from God? Who knows our *downsitting* and our *uprising*? Who understands our thoughts afar off and acquainted with all our ways? There is no hiding place no matter how we try! Adam and Eve tried it and was found naked.

My days of running away from the Lord are over, thank God! No one else could take the sin and darkness from me but Jesus! No one else could have caused such amazing transformation in my life from the path of self-destruction to a life of renewed hope of eternal life!

A Declaration of Fact from a Well-Renowned King

Once upon a time, there was a well-renowned king by the name of Nebuchadnezzar who declared that three of his subjects should be put to death in a fiery furnace for not obeying his decree to worship his golden image. These three God-fearing young men—Shadrach, Meshach, and Abednego—decided that they would rather die a martyr's death than to renounce their faith in the God of their fathers, Abraham, Isaac, and Jacob. They refused to fall down and worship false god and the golden image as the king demanded. Because of the love and allegiance they had for the one true God, they were bound and cast into the fiery furnace. Nevertheless, they were kept alive by the Son of God who accompanied them into the furnace, God's divine intervention. Henceforth, the king confessed and declared, "there is no other God that can deliver after this sort" (Dan. 3:29).

This same God delivered me from death and despair while I was on my knees, praying the Sinner's Prayer. As I prayed, "Lord, have mercy on my soul," at that very moment, an awesome miraculous act of salvation took place in my life. My life has never been the same since.

A Man after God's Own Heart

The psalmist David, declared:

> *Whither shall I go from thy spirit? or whither shall I flee from thy presence? If I ascend to heaven, thou art there: if I make my bed in hell, behold, thou art there. If I take the winds of the morning, and dwell in the uttermost parts of the sea; Even there shall thy hand lead me, and thy right hand shall hold me. (Ps. 139:7–10)*

Man's Inborn Desire

The inborn desire of men from birth to the grave are always goal-oriented. Some people desire lofty goals. Others may set goals to live the life they love and love the life they live. By doing so, they are hiding themselves from their Creator by their denial of his absolute Lordship over them.

However, if any of my readers love the life they live and live the life they love, in the end at the day of reckoning, decide to hide from his or her Creator, that will not work, not even if you should resort to this well-known adage, "If you want to jump over a fence and aim for the treetop, you may not clear the fence. However, if you aim for the moon, you're bound to clear the fence!" That may be true, however, even if you reach the moon, you will not escape the presence of God.

Over thirty-five years ago, my life was one of hardship and despair, running away from God, my Creator. But the Lord knew just where to find me. For it is written, "Behold, I have graven thee upon the palms of my hands; thy walls are continually before me" (Isa. 49:16).

A Tuesday Afternoon

On a Tuesday afternoon in the year 1964, I was taking a nap on my father's bed. As usual, I always get down on my knees and pray before I go to bed. That afternoon, something happened. This event is explained in my book, *From the Brink of Suicide* when a wonderful change took place in my life for all eternity! *A life is a precious thing to waste!*

A Personal View of Creation

Just look at yourself in the mirror. You will see the product of God's creation—a unique you! Thank God, you and I are able to tell the beautiful product of God's creation! You are blessed with a brain, the organ of thought enclosed in the skull and upper cerebral cortex. All the organs are important, however, without the brain and the heart that pumps the circulation of the blood, we are physically dead.

Now let's talk about life and beauty. Isn't it good and pleasant to talk about the beautiful and lovely things God made? The botanical garden, especially at springtime in the tropics, when all the flowers raise their lovely heads in full blossom is such radiant beauty that thrills the hearts of your wives and loved ones.

Christ described the significance and beauty of flowers. He emphasized on the lilies of the field, "That even Solomon in all his glory was not arrayed like one of these" (Matt. 6:29). Everything that God created subjected freely to his will, except mankind. How sweet is the smell of the full-bloom roses that thrill the hearts of women when presented in love! Only a super intelligent God could create such a unique form of creation.

An Act of Thanksgiving versus an Unthankful Heart

Despite all these things, there are those poor individuals who do not find it necessary to give thanks to the Creator, the one who has provided so many good gifts and blessings for all living things to enjoy!

Most people don't find it necessary to say thank you for a new day, not realizing it was their Creator who has kept them safe through the night and all day long. Have you ever experience when you said good morning only to receive a sarcastic remark, "What's so good about the morning?" Had it not been for the grace of God, he or she would not be able to see the morning light.

There is no exception to the act of thanksgiving. A perfect example of a thankful heart is Jesus, the Son of God. In many occasions, we read of Jesus giving thanks to his heavenly Father. "The servant is not greater than his lord" (Jn. 15:20). Therefore, if Christ found it necessary to give thanks to his heavenly Father, how much more should we, his servants, give thanks.

I am reminded of a situation while I was walking down 149th street in the Bronx, I saw a homeless man rummaging through garbage cans, looking for food. I offered him some loose change I had in my pocket. The man refused to accept my offer. That is one example of an unthankful heart.

Not so long ago, there was a banality expressed in our society, "Brother, can you spare a dime?" The solution to this segment of our society, however, is charity with the incentive to help oneself. Allow me to refer you to this popular proverb, "Give a man a fish and he will feed himself for a day. Teach him how to fish and he will feed himself and his family for the rest of his life!"

7

OUR UNIQUE EARTH

Earth is the fifth largest planet of the solar system, the only one known to support life. The change of seasons is caused by the 23.5-degree tilt of the Earth's axis to the plane of its orbit. Earth's atmosphere, made up mostly oxygen and nitrogen gases surrounds the planet. Studies indicate that the Earth consists of concentric layers that differ in size, chemistry, and density. At the center of our planet is an outer core believed to be liquid and an inner solid core. Earth is alleged to be about 4.5 billion years old; its origin is a controversial subject. Earth has one natural satellite, the moon.

Planets are, according to astronomers, any relatively large, nonluminous bodies that revolve around the sun. Solar system the sun and the family of planets: natural satellites, asteroids, meteors, and comets that are its captives, according to astronomers. The principal members of the retinue of the sun are the nine major planets, in order of increasing distance from the sun, they are Mercury, Venus, Earth, Mars, Jupiter, Saturn, Uranus, Neptune, and Pluto. The planets orbit the sun in approximately the same plane (elliptic) and move in the same direction (west to east). Current theories suggest that the solar system was formed from a nebula consisting of a dense nucleus or protosun, surrounded by a thin shell of a gaseous matter extending to the present edges of the solar system. This, however, is man's assumption, most of which is supported by probability, not facts! Earth, as we know it today, is without question the most unique planet in all of God's creation!

Thousands of years since man began his epic journey to search for new frontiers in the outer limits of space, communications was at its zenith as all the people of the earth were united in their effort and aspired to accomplish every imagination of their heart because they had only one language, until the fall of the tower of Babel. Henceforth, an evil thought entered into the heart of their leader. Emperor Nimrod, desiring to broaden his horizon, increase his overall knowledge, and widen his frontiers beyond the boundaries of earth. He amassed the most brilliant scientist, engineers, craftsmen and able-bodied men and women to accomplish his lofty goals by erecting a gigantic tower that would reach the heavens above.

The omniscient God who is all-knowing, knew their thoughts, that it was deceitful and desperately wicked. He would not permit such breach of his sovereignty so God confounded their language so they could not understand each other. "Every kingdom divided against itself is brought to desolation; and every city or house divided against itself shall not stand" (Matt. 12:25). Henceforth, man was scattered upon the face of the earth because he no longer had a common language to unite him in his quest for knowledge and power (Gen. 11:6–9). Only the omnipotent God of all creation, with his mighty acts, can work such awesome wonder!

Cosmology

The science that aims at a comprehensive theory of the creation, evolution, and present structure of the entire universe. The Ptolemaic system and the Copernican system are theories that describe the position of Earth in the universe.

By studying the distribution of star clusters, Harlow Shapley gave the first reliable estimate of the size of our galaxy (100,000 light-years) and of the position of the sun within it (30-000 light-years from the center). The big bang theory states that all of the matter and energy in the universe was concentrated in a very small volume that exploded between ten and twenty billion years ago and that the resulting expansion allegedly continues today! The strongest evidence for the big bang theory is the feeble radio background radiation discovered in the 1960s that is received from every part of the sky. How homogeneous early universe implied by the uniform background radiation evolved into the present universe of cluster and superclusters of galaxies separated by enormous voids remain unanswered. As does the question of whether the universe will continue or eventually halt and reverse, with the universe collapsing in the so-called big crunch.

According to another hypothesis, the steady state theory, the universe expands but new matter is continuously created at all points in space left by the receding galaxies. This theory now has few adherents. Because the Genesis account of Creation is overwhelmingly convincing, the cosmologists may hypothesize. The word of God, nevertheless, holds preeminence over man's finite ability to comprehend the mystery of God's creation of the earth and the universe, a belief espoused by all true Bible-believing Christians. The Darwinist theory of evolution is an unproven fallacy in comparison to the biblical account of creation and has been substantiated by factual evidence, including recent and ongoing archeological findings!

I'm not a product of Ardipithecus ramidus, a hominoid species alleged to have chimpanzee-like form assumed by the evolutionist to be our first ancestor 4.4 million years ago. The first fossil was discovered in 1922, the most primitive hominid yet found. They may have walked upright and lived in the forest. I can say with absolute certainty that I am not a byproduct of Australopithecus anamensis that exhibit some characteristics of primitive hominids that walked on two feet 4.2 to 3.9 million years ago. I am a living human being made in the image of my Creator with soul, body, and spirit now washed in his blood.

How ironic and presumptuous it is for man to discount the Bible's account of creation, choosing rather to rely on the inaccurate findings and conclusion of carbon dating to determine the approximate age of objects. When and where do men obtain the knowledge to scientifically calculate the dates and origins of these objects? In addition, how long did it take finite minds to study and acquire this knowledge? The approximate eighteen years or more of research and learning that it takes to acquire the knowledge to conceive the thought and idea of the big bang theory of evolution is a very long time. In comparison to the Creator who just spoke the earth and universe into existence faster than the speed of light, it takes the idea of the big bang theory to materialize. How long did it take the Lord to complete his Creation? It took the Lord six days to complete his creation. All that he did was spoke the word, "Let there be light!" and there was light. Can mortal man do the same? The challenge is out for anyone who dares to say yes.

Let us consider for a moment light traveling at the speed of 186,000 miles per second, from a distance of 100,000 light-years away from our galaxy and the position of the sun within it (30,000 light-years from the center). Such calculation boggles the mind, not so with the Creator. He said let there be light and there was light, not 100,000 light-years later at the relatively slow rate. Therefore, to compete with or to deny the existence of this supernatural power is a futile attempt.

Man Being the Student of History

As a student of history, man attempts to exhibit more knowledge than the greatest teacher of all creation!

For those who chose to believe and embrace the theory of evolution as facts, rather than the overwhelming evidence and the word of the one true God of all creation, consider the inspired words of Apostle Paul who writes, "For in him we live, and move, and have our being; as certain also of your own poets have said, For we are also his offspring. Forasmuch then as we are the offspring of God, we ought not to think the Godhead is like unto gold, or silver, or stone, graven by art and man's device" (Acts 17:28–29). We are not the offspring of ape and chimpanzees! "And the times of this ignorance God winked at; but now commandeth all men every where to repent" (Acts. 17:30).

When King Nebuchadnezzar commanded that all should fall down and worship his image of gold as god, Shadrach, Meshach, and Abednego refused. Their refusal to worship a false god resulted in them being thrown into a fiery furnace (Dan. 3:1–30).

Even more profound declaration by our Lord and Savior reads thus, "And that servant, which knew his lord's will, and prepared not himself, neither did according to this will, shall be beaten with many stripes" (Lk. 12:47). Thus said the word of the Lord, the Creator and Savior of the world!

Archaic Homo sapiens

Alleged Homo sapiens belong to an earlier time. Fossil remains of archaic Homo sapiens were found in Africa and Europe in 5000,000 to 200,000 years ago, First fossil found in 1921. [Assumed, not fact]!

During my moments of reflections, a question came to mind. How is it that archeologists and anthropologists never found our ancestors (Adam and Eve, Enoch, Moses, and Elijah) or the remains of Christ? For obvious reasons, it is impossible because we know from the Scriptures where these men are today. Christ, for example, is our resurrected Savior and is now seated on his throne at the right hand of the Father! "Enoch walked with God: and he was not; for God took him (up to heaven)" (Gen. 5:24, emphasis added). The body of Moses was buried by God. Later in the New Testament, he appeared on the mount of transfiguration with Jesus and Elias (Matt. 17:3). So archeologists and anthropologists will never find the remains of these men. Not in this life, I hasten to add.

Forensic experts, in conjunction with the anthropologists and the evolutionists, may persuasively argue their case on behalf of Darwin's theory of evolution. Nevertheless, they are not able to convince the majority of believers by their findings that we evolved from apes and chimpanzees. The truth is, man is made in the image of God our Creator, not from apes and chimps. We are not the products of randomly selective mutation as the evolutionist would have us to believe. We are the offspring of created human, not animals.

The Embodiment of Meekness

Moses, described in the Bible as the meekest man on earth, had his weaknesses. But God imputed unto him his righteousness. God took Moses home where he died on the Mount Nebo and was buried in a valley in the land of Moab, "but no man knoweth of his sepulcher unto this day" (Deut. 34:6). Moses and Elias appeared on the mount of transfiguration with Jesus and three of his disciples. Only the Creator can perform such supernatural transformation of human life. That, however, was not the result of selective mutation that the evolutionist assumed as facts. Henceforth, whose report and credibility will you trust, man's or God's?

We are just sojourners and pilgrims here on this earth, awaiting a better home. "For he looked for a city which hath foundations, whose builder and maker is God" (Heb. 11:10). Before these men were taken away to be with the Lord, I thought perhaps they desired a better country "that is, an heavenly, wherefore God is not ashamed to be called their God: for he hath prepared for them a city" (Heb. 11:16). What better company to be in than with Jesus? The mount of transfiguration was a perfect example of the promise of sovereign grace and love toward us, "God having provided some better things for us" (Heb. 11:40).

My personal experience and relationship with the Lord is explained in my book, *From the Brink of Suicide*. By all accounts, God has proven himself time and time again to be the only true wise God, the Creator of heaven and earth and of all things. Who else could make all these things possible? Only the true and living God can. He alone is Lord of all.

8

Hominid Fills Gap in Fossil Record

Alleged reconstructive artistry of 2.5 million years old fossil skull may resemble ancient human remains unlike that of our first parents. Believers of the Bible's account of God, Adam, and Creation, have been resolute in our belief and allegiance to our Creator. We are not the products of evolution, we are the offspring of his marvelous creation.

Jesus is the author and finisher of our faith, the Scripture emphatically said. In the beginning, God created the heaven and the earth. "And God created great whales, and every living creature that moveth" (Gen. 1:21). These are proven facts that does not need man's approval and validation. God, our Creator, has declared, "Let the earth bring forth the living creature after his kind, cattle, and creeping things, and beast of the earth after his kind: and it was so. And God made the beast of the earth after his kind, and cattle after their kind, and every thing that creeps upon the earth after his kind: and God saw that it was good" (Gen. 1:24–25).

Who in their right mind can argue with the omnipotent God of all creations and win? History is full of men and women who have attempted such folly and have failed big time. Nimrod tried it at the tower of Babel and was found wanting. God confounded his knowledge along with his followers.

Finite Man versus the Infinite Creator

Finite man against the infinite Creator, there is no comparison. After Daniel, the man of God, told Nebuchadnezzar, the king of Babylon, the interpretation of his dream, he found out his place in history, according to God's timetable was in order to fulfill his purpose, not the far-fetched heresy of the evolutionists whose assumption is that we are the products of natural selection.

According to Daniel 4:29, "At the end of twelve months, he walked in the kingdom of Babylon." As always, note the arrogance of man when he chose to walk outside the will of God. "The king spake, and said, Is not this great Babylon, that I have built for the house of the kingdom by the might of my power, and for the honour of my majesty?" (Dan. 4:30). While men speak boastfully, God always has the final say in everything we say and do! "While the word was in the king's mouth, there fell a voice from heaven, saying, O king Nebuchadnezzar, to thee it is spoken; The kingdom is departed from thee" (Dan. 4:31). Because Christ is always merciful, men have a chance to repent and make a comeback as long as they plead for mercy. Daniel 4:32 reads, "they shall make thee to eat grass as oxen, and seven times shall pass over thee, until thou know that the most High ruleth in the kingdom of men, and giveth it to whomsoever he will." God does not make idle threats. Whatever he says, he will do. He always does. "The same hour was the thing fulfilled upon Nebuchadnezzar: and he was driven from men, and did eat grass as oxen, and his body was wet with the dew of heaven, till his hairs were grown like eagles' feathers, and his nails like birds' claw" (Dan. 4:33). No one, who truly experiences an extraordinary encounter with God can honestly deny the power and existence of the Creator. "And at the end of days I Nebuchadnezzar lifted up mine eyes unto heaven, and mine understanding returned unto me, and I blessed the most High, and I praised and honoured him that liveth for ever, whose dominion is an everlasting dominion, and his kingdom is from generation to generation" (Dan. 4:34).

Adherence to the truth versus assumed fact is a lesson the evolutionist and all those who deny the existence of the Creator might do well to learn from the examples of history. No one who truly experiences an extraordinary encounter with God can honestly deny the power and existence of the Creator.

Testimonial of a Remorseful Man

"And all the inhabitants of the earth are reputed as nothing: and he doeth according to his will in the army of heaven, and among the inhabitants of the earth: and none can stay his hand, or say unto him, What doest thou?" (Dan. 4:35). Reason was restored to King Nebuchadnezzar after expressing genuine remorse and confessing his folly in regard to the existence of God. Daniel 4:36 reads, "At the same time my reason returned unto me; and for the glory of my kingdom, mine honour and brightness returned unto me; and my counselors and my lords sought unto me; and I was established in my kingdom, and excellent majesty was added unto me." Confession and praise to the only true God continued as King Nebuchadnezzar made his confession. "Now I Nebuchadnezzar praise and extol and honour the King of heaven, all whose words are truth and his ways judgment: and those that walk in pride he is able to abase" (Dan. 4:37).

No One Ever Wins an Argument with God

History has shown that no one no one ever argues with God and wins. The pharaoh of Egypt tried to argue his case and imitate the miracles of God through his servants Moses and Aaron. However, they failed in their attempts to create lice from the dust of the ground. Only God can create life from the dust of the ground (Gen. 2:7, Exod. 8:17–18).

An insincere confession, unlike that of Nebuchadnezzar, is unacceptable. [Verse 19] reads. "Then the magicians said unto Pharaoh, This is the finger of God: and Pharaoh's heart was hardened, and he harkened not unto them; as the Lord has said" (Exod. 8:19).

Alleged assumption, not facts, is the evidence the evolutionist has presented in his counterarguments of creation. They keep coming up with unproven theory of evolution, which cannot be proven as fact. They claim that life evolved through natural selection of the species. They failed to realize that these organisms came from somewhere in the first place. Don't they know that God is the author and finisher of our faith and of all things from the beginning to the end? "All things were made by him; and without him was not any thing made that was made" (Jn. 1:3).

According to the big bang theory, light travels at the speed of 186,000 miles per second, 100,000 light-years from the center of our galaxy from the moment of the alleged big bang theory. However, our planet, including the hundreds of billions of stars in our galaxy, would still be hurtling through space. Destination unknown! Thank God for the creation of our planet by God the Creator who spoke the world into existence, including the sun, moon, and stars. "And God said, Let there be light: and there was light" (Gen. 1:3). In six days, the entire creation was completed. The Lord could have done it all in one day if he wanted to. Nevertheless, he took six days, and on the seventh day He rested, according to his divine purpose.

Kingdom of the Seahorse

Of all males in the animal kingdom, only one can be sure of his paternity. That animal is the seahorse. With seahorses, it is the male—and only the male—who gets pregnant and gives birth. Their extraordinary looks and surprising behavior have earned them a mythic stature, one that now puts them in peril. Millions are slaughtered each year and used in Chinese medicine as cure for impotence.

Tony Kahan A pregnant Seahorse from the study sites has given birth. According to the article, Amanda's team takes particular care with the tiny offspring, for these babies are unlike any in the world. They were born from a pregnant male like this one. Over the course of the breeding season, this seahorse will father [allegedly] over a thousand young, all nurtured within his body. The male seahorse is distinguished from the female by a pouch, which acts as a womb. The male gets pregnant and gives birth. However, to learn more about Seahorse parenting, takes patience.

Amanda Vincent said, "A lot of people find it really difficult to believe me when I say it's the males that get pregnant! I think that it is because we are mammals and mammals, by definition, the females carry the young! Which raises a whole interesting perspective that we have to think about, whether the roles of males and females are permanent and fixed or whether, in fact, there is a lot of flexibility."

With all due respect to Adam Vincent, the truth is, the only flexibility required as it relates to the inerrancy of the word of the Creator. With regard to the difference between the male and female gender, strict adherence to the word of the Creator declared in Genesis 3:15–16. "Heaven and earth shall pass away, but my words shall not pass away" (Matt. 24:35).

During the process of writing this chapter, I took a brief moment from my research to ponder on what would be the appropriate note on which to conclude this chapter. Then I came across the title of the subject in question.

Kingdom of the Seahorse:

Article reads:

> As quoted previously of all males in the animal kingdom, only one can be sure of his paternity. That animal is the Seahorse. Only because in Seahorse, it is the male, and only the male, who gets pregnant and gives birth.

Was there a moment of fear of standing on spiritual quicksand when I came across this article? Absolutely not! Because Christ is my rock I stand on, all other ground is sinking sand. Therefore, I would like to refer you directly to the one whose credibility outweighs all others in every questionable situation that may arise. Therefore, this is the question the Creator asked mankind, "Ask ye now, and see whether a man doeth travail with child? wherefore do I see every man with his hands on his loins, as a woman in travail, and all faces are turned into paleness?" (Jer. 30:6). Whose credibility will you believe? Man has flawed credibility, which brings us back to the previous statements, *history shows that no one ever wins an argument with God.*

Although I am not an expert in the study of biological science, nevertheless, from my understanding and belief in the word of the Creator, he created man and woman in his own image. He created them male and female so that they would procreate and bring forth children of the human race from their union.

The Procreation Promise Continued

With Noah, his wife, three sons, and their wives, only eight souls were saved from that great flood! Prior to the great flood, God instructed Noah to build an ark for himself and his family and to warn the people of their impending doom. During the hundred and twenty years it took Noah to build the ark, he preached the message of repentance to all—small and great, rich and poor—until the day the flood came and destroyed them all. God also told Noah to gather into the ark a pair of every animal, male and female after their kind! That was an example of God preserving the species and the human race.

With all due respect to the researchers, the word of the Creator is final in its entirety regarding the subject of male and female species for procreation in both animals and human.

9

Human Love versus Instinctive Love in the Animal Species

True love from the human race is unlike that of the animal species! Most adult in the animal species instinctively protect their young. Similarly, humans have the greater propensity to love with passion no other creature has. Man and woman were created in the image of God with the capacity to love and forgive, an ability the animal species does not have for sure.

Despite man's propensity to love notwithstanding, because of sin, he is still capable to hate and exhibit selfish characteristics. "Looking out for number one" is the motto of the selfish, an attitude that in permeates the hearts and minds of today's society.

Case in point, during the summer of July 1999 in New York City, we had that sudden drench of torrential rainfall for about three hours, which caused this great metropolis' subway system to come to a grinding halt. Practically all subways and rail systems were inoperable because of the severe flooding. Suddenly, out of the chaos emerged the display the me-first attitude. *Looking out for number one.* The subway was bustling with cell phone activity, transmitting messages to employers, friends, and loved ones and informing them of the inconveniences and unexpected delay. Everyone was pushing and shoving to get on the available buses to get to their destinations.

Thus, the human heart with its capacity and propensity to love, to hate, and to forgive was at its zenith!

The Human Cry

The human cry from a selfish heart was the worse behavior we have seen and heard loud and clear as we got on the packed bus. "Go express! Go express! All the way downtown!" were the shouts echoed by many of the passengers. How could anyone forget so quickly that they were also outside waiting in the rain to get on board? When the bus eventually came to a particular stop to drop off and pick up other passengers, there was an individual passenger who came on the bus. She too was urging the driver to go all the way downtown while others were still outside in the rain, waiting to get on. This individual demonstrated the me-first behavioral pattern, forgetting that she too was struggling to get out of the rain a short time ago.

This should be a reminder to us all. No matter what position one holds in life, whether you are a straphanger or a successful pastor of a very large church with a humble beginning, you have the power to help a potential member of your church. It is within your power to help those individuals who were called by God and need to be encouraged with moral and spiritual support from their leaders. Therefore, those who are in the position of power and influence to help their fellowmen, especially those of the household of faith, failing to do so is an abomination to God! Let us not forget the Golden Rule, "Therefore all things whatsoever ye would that men should do to you, do ye even so to them: for this is the law and the prophets" (Matt. 7:12).

The above illustration demonstrates the behavioral tendency and capacity of the human heart to love and to hate, to share and to forgive. Some have shown that not all of us were uncaring and unkind. Indeed, some of us were genuinely courteous to each other. The foregoing examples not only apply to straphangers and ordinary individuals, but to all concerned. Whether you are a man of the clergy, a straphanger, or whatever your field of occupation may be, the general truth applies. "Do unto others as you would like them to do unto you."

Based on the past and present experiences, it would not be difficult to write a book on this subject alone. We know that our hope is built on the incorruptible promises of Jehovah-jireh (the Lord will provide), not on what man can and cannot do for who can shut an open door in the face of God's elect. "Nevertheless the foundation of God standeth sure, having this seal, The Lord knoweth them that are his. And, let every one that nameth the name of Christ depart from iniquity" (2 Tim. 2:19).

The Golden Rule Principles

In addition to the aforementioned Golden Rule, "Do unto others as you would like them to do unto you," the next example was a scene in a divorce court drama on TV. The drama unfolded during the course of the show.

There was this estranged couple who was contesting each other's claim. Their contentious charges and countercharges became so embroiled that the judge intervened and asked the estranged wife what she did for a living and where she worked. "The library," she replied. The judge asked, "Aren't there any books there in the library that you can read to help you in your marriage?" The husband interjected, suggesting the Bible as a good book. The judge concurred, "I think that is a good book to read!" The judge then asked the husband, "Do you read it?" He answered, "Yes, Your Honor! I read it every day. I live by it every day."

How presumptuous it is for an individual to make such claim as to live by the Bible's Golden Rule every day while, out of the same mouth, came forth lying, cursing, swearing, and openly criticizing each other vehemently, which was and is a very poor standard by which to represent God's principle of the Golden Rule.

Unpleasant Mixture

The unpleasant mixture of bitter and sweet water coming from the same fountain is not the norm. James was inspired to write, "Doth a fountain send forth at the same place sweet water and bitter? Can the fig tree, my brethren, bear olive berries? either a vine, figs? So can no fountain both yield salt water and fresh" (Jas. 3:11–12).

Oh, come on now, Simeon! Lighten up! Get real! How about hybrid grafting of agricultural food chain?" That may be so. However, genetic engineering of plant life is contrary to nature, not the natural way of seedtime and harvest as the scripture declared. "While the earth remaineth, seedtime and harvest, and cold and heat, and summer and winter, and day and night shall not cease" (Gen. 8:22).

Getting back to the subject of James' exposition of abnormal mixture of bitter and sweet water coming from the same fountain, James 3:13–16 reads, "Who is a wise man and imbued with knowledge among you? let him shew out of a good conversation his works with meekness of wisdom. But if ye have bitter envying and strife in your hearts, glory not, and lie not against the truth. This wisdom descendeth not from above, but is earthly, sensual, devilish. For where envying and strife is, there is confusion and every evil work" Anyone who professes to know the Lord but do not demonstrate a change life or behavior is not wise. "But the wisdom that is from above is first pure, then peaceable, gentle, and easy to be intreated, full of mercy and good fruits, without partiality, and without hypocrisy. And the fruit of righteousness is sown in peace of them that make peace" (Jas. 3:17–18). Thus, the opening statement of a fountain with sweet and bitter water means a changed life and a changed attitude.

The Philosophical Standard of Truth

Psychology for Better Living states that philosophy may be considered as a person's formal or informal, ordered or disordered, consistent or inconsistent, and conscious or unconscious assumptions about the nature of truth.

Quoting from the above statement, "First, it must be understood that truth is a relative rather than a concrete concept. [Says who?] Most students assume that truth is a property like length, which can be objectively measured, and that everyone will agree on the outcome. Truth, unlike length, has no agreed upon measuring standards."

What is Truth?

When Jesus was asked of his true identity, "Art thou a king?" Jesus answered, "Thou sayest that I am a king. To this end was I born, and for this cause came I into the world, that I should witness unto the truth. Every one that is of the truth heareth my voice. Pilate saith unto him, What is truth? And when he hath said this, he went out again unto the Jews, and saith unto them, I find in him no fault at all" (Jn. 18:37–38).

Therefore, you may try to bend the truth, stretch it, go around it, fly over it, or set goals to circumvent it. However, try if you may, you will not succeed. This reminds me of a unique quotation regarding setting realistic or unrealistic goals. "If you want to jump over a fence and aim for the treetop, you may not clear the fence. But if you aim for the moon, you're bound to clear the fence!" Even though there may be some smidgen of truth to the above quotation, nevertheless, in your vain effort to circumvent the truth, you will realize you cannot bend it, cross over it, go around it, jump over it, or fly over it. Neither can you go through it except through Christ. Jesus said, "I am the way, the truth, and the life: no man cometh unto the Father, but by me" (Jn. 14:6). Man's philosophy of truth may vary according to the theory of relativity, however, God's truth is absolute and unvarying.

10

WISDOM VERSUS PHILOSOPHY

The dictionary defines *wisdom* as:

1. accumulated learning,
2. good sense,
3. the body of things known about,
4. or information, lore, and science.

Solomon, the wisest man throughout all generations, defines wisdom as the following. "A wise man will hear, and will increase learning; and a man of understanding shall attain unto wise counsels... The fear of the Lord is the beginning of knowledge: but fools despise wisdom and instruction" (Prov. 1:5,7). "Wait just a minute, all that is just Bible talk. Get a life!" You may ask, "How about all the geniuses and computer wizards of our time?"

I do acknowledge the enormous progress we have made in our time through the increase of knowledge especially in the areas of science and engineering, printed and electronics communications, medical diagnostics and research (magnetic resonance imaging or MRI and nuclear magnetic resonance or NMR), and many others too numerous to mention. The "nuclear" in NMR is unlike the atomic energy used in nuclear explosion. The term refers to the nucleus of the cell in a tissue. Whose report will you believe, man's interpretation of wisdom or the words of the inspired author, the wisest mortal that ever lived? You notice I use the word *mortal* to describe man with the understanding that Christ is the Creator of all wisdom, knowledge, and understanding.

Philosophy, on the other hand, is the study of fundamental beliefs, science, liberal arts—exclusive of medicine, law, and theology—and the system of ideas, sum of personal convictions and calmness. Philosophically speaking, hasn't the world given us this kind of teaching throughout the history of civilization and the end result scares society? The Greeks, for example, represent love of wisdom. But whose wisdom, man's or the Creators definition of wisdom? In Greek philosophy, wisdom is the study of the ultimate reality, cause, and principle underlying being and thinking. Western philosophy, dating from 600 BC when the Greeks established inquiry independent of theological creeds, is traditionally divided into approximately five major branches. God, however, is the ultimate source of all wisdom, knowledge, and understanding.

Among the five major branches of the Greeks theological creeds are:

- *Metaphysics.* Metaphysics look into the nature and ultimate significance of the universe, holding reality to subsist in thought. Nevertheless, the word of God said, "For that they hated knowledge, and did not chose the fear of the Lord: They would none of my council: they despised all my reproof" (Prov. 1:29–30).

- *Idealism.* Idealism deals with matters, adherence to ideas, and tendency to see things in matters of materialism or in both dualism and materialism. The theory that matter is the only reality, preoccupation with material, and not spiritual. This, however, is a typical tendency of man, always wanting to have things his way. "There is a way that seemeth right unto a man, but the end thereof are the ways of death" (Prov. 16:25). So was the case for Adam and Eve in the beginning. It must be emphasized, however, that Jesus is the only way to life everlasting. "The thief commeth not, but for to steal, and to kill, and to destroy, I am come that they might have life, and that they might have it more abundantly" (Jn. 10:10).

God has given to every man the free will to choose, therefore choose life and not the ways of death, which is the alternative of doing things your way.

Moses, who was a great expositor of God's word, commanded Israel in this manner, "I call heaven and earth to record this day against you, that I have set before you life and death, blessing and cursing: therefore choose life, that both thou and thy seed may live" (Deut. 30:19).

This is a sharp contrast to *idealism*, which deals with matter adhering to ideas and tendency to see things as they should be, instead of seeing things God's way, regardless of how well intended the philosophy of idealism is. Good works, no matter how well intentioned, will not guarantee assurance of eternal life. Jesus said, "I am the way, the truth, and the life, no man cometh unto the Father, but by me" (Jn. 14:6).

- *Logic.* Logic is the science of sound reasoning and is concerned with the laws of valid reasoning. However, let us clarify a more candid and unambiguous explanation of the logic of sound reasoning. According to the supernatural intelligence of the omniscient, notice what he has to say about logic and reasoning as we adhere to what the Lord said.

"Come now, and let us reason together, saith the Lord: though your sins be as scarlet, they shall be as white as snow; though they be red like crimson, they shall be as wool. If ye be willing and obedient, ye shall eat the good of the land: But if you refused and rebel, ye shall be devoured with the sword: for the mouth of the Lord hath spoken it" (Isa. 1:18–20). This is the true definition of sound logic, perceived directly and understood by almost all true Bible-believing Christians.

- *Epistemology.* Among the Greek philosophy is *epistemology*, which investigates the nature of knowledge and the process of knowing. By knowing, we mean "to perceive directly or understand." It is written, "But the natural man receiveth not the things of the Spirit of God: for they are foolishness unto him" (1 Cor. 2:14). Therefore, unless the Father draws man to Jesus, the Son of God, they would not be able to understand the call of God in their life. That is why Isaiah the prophet was inspired to write, "Who hath believed our report? and to whom is the arm of the Lord revealed?" (Isa. 53:1).

Thorough knowledge comes not from man's understanding, but from knowing who is the author and finisher of our faith.

> *My son, if thou wilt receive my words, and hide my commandments with thee; So that thou incline thine ear unto wisdom, and apply thine heart to understanding; Yea, if thou criest after knowledge, and liftest up thy voice for understanding; If thou seekest her as silver, and searches for her as for hid treasures; Then shalt thou understand the fear of the Lord, and find the knowledge of God. For the Lord giveth wisdom: out of his mouth commeth knowledge and understanding. (Prov. 2:1–6)*

- *Ethics.* The philosophy of ethics deals with the problems of right conduct. However, that cannot be achieved without the spirit of Christ dwelling in one's heart by conversion. In this day and age of political correctness, where every person deals with the issue of right or wrong in their own way, where the issues of right and wrong and dos and donts are no longer relevant from a moral and biblical point of view. It is not fashionable, even from a great many pulpits, to speak or emphasize on the subject of holiness anymore, fearing that they might offend someone and be labeled as being a judgmental, holier-than-thou holy rollers.

Let us be reminded that the prosperity, which most of us have come to enjoy today from a booming economy, did not come about through intimidation or what others may have thought about us in a negative way. All of this prosperity came about through hard work, intercessory prayers of godly people, and innovative ideas. Hundreds of thousands have given their lives to protect the sovereignty of this great nation so that we all can enjoy the wealth and prosperity that most of us have today.

Our founding fathers were not afraid to express their views that freedom of religion is an integral part of our constitution. It written in the first amendment in the Declaration of Independence, "that all men are created equal, that they are endowed by their Creator with certain inalienable Rights, that among these are life, liberty, and the pursuit of happiness." So by expressing those views, it clearly indicates that they were not afraid to confess faith in their Creator. Therefore, their Creator expects no lesser sacrifice from us but to live godly, happy, and ethical lives by his Spirit.

Think of all the martyrs who have given their lives for the gospel of the kingdom of God so that men and women may have the freedom to worship God in spirit and in truth without fear of being labeled as judgmental "holy rollers." By all accounts, their actions demonstrated their convictions, not their fears! "For God hath not given us the spirit of fear; but of power, and of love, and of a sound mind. Be not thou therefore ashamed of the testimony of our Lord, nor of me his prisoner: but be thou partaker of the afflictions of the gospel according to the power of God" (2 Tim. 1:7–8).

Therefore, why should today's Christian be subject to a lesser standard of faithfulness? For goodness sake, let's not return to those days when every imagination of man's heart was only evil continually that caused the wrath of God's visitation upon the sins of man (Gen. 6:5).

Historically, philosophy has fallen into three major periods: ancient, medieval, and modern. Philosophy emphasized a concern with the ultimate nature of reality and the problem of virtue in a political context. Most of the problems of philosophy, according to history, were defined by the Greeks. Socrates, Plato, and Aristotle were the towering figures of classical philosophy. Medieval philosophy in the west was virtually inseparable from Christian thought. For that reason, it is written:

Let not mercy and truth forsake thee: bind them about thy neck; write them upon the table of thine heart: So shalt thou find favour and good understanding in the sight of God and man. Trust in the Lord with all thine heart; and lean not unto thine own understanding. In all thy ways acknowledge him, and he shall direct your paths. (Prov. 3:3–6)

However well intended his views were and somewhat misguided by his philosophy, Socrates was equating virtue with knowledge of one's true self, saying that no one knowingly does wrong, when the scripture emphatically said, "And God saw that the wickedness of man was great in the earth, and that every thoughts of his heart was only evil continually" (Gen. 6:5). That is why the word of God said, "Trust in the Lord with all thine heart; and lean not unto thine own understanding. In all thy ways acknowledge him, and he shall direct thy paths" (Prov. 3:5–6).

If Socrates had solemnly committed to this doctrine, he would not have held such heretical views that no one knowingly does wrong. Such heretical views are the antithesis of what God said in Genesis 6:5.

Socrates

Socrates (469–399 BC) was Greek philosopher of Athens and generally regarded as one of the wisest people of all times. Socrates himself left no writings. Most of our knowledge of him and his teachings comes from the dialogues of his most famous pupil Plato and from memories of Xenophon.

Socrates is described as having neglected his own affairs, choosing instead to spend his time discussing virtue, justice, and piety wherever his fellow citizens congregated, seeking wisdom about right conduct so that he might guide the moral and intellectual improvement of Athens. His criticism of the Sophists and of Athenians political and religious institutions made him many enemies. Among them was Aristophanes. In 399 BC, Socrates was tried for corrupting the morals of Athenian youth and for religious heresies. It is now believed that his arrest stemmed, in particular, from his influence on Alcibiades and Critias who betrayed Athens. He was convicted. Resisting all efforts to save his life, he willingly drank the cup of poison hemlock given to him.

In the *Apology of Socrates*, *Crito*, and *Phaedo*, Plato describes the trial and death of Socrates. At this time, I would like to interject the inspired words of Peter,

> *For this is thankworthy, if a man for conscience toward God endure grief, suffering wrongfully. For what glory is it, if, when you be buffeted for your faults, ye shall take it patiently? but if, when ye do well, and suffer for it, ye take it patiently, this is acceptable with God. For even hereunto were ye called: because Christ also suffered for us, leaving us an example, that ye should follow in his steps. (1 Pet. 2:19–21)*

Socrates may have established good moral virtues. However, good work cannot save anyone. "For by grace are you saved through faith; and that not of yourselves: it is the gift of God: Not of works, lest any man should boast" (Eph. 2:8–9).

Man's Standards

Man has always needed recognition from others. He likes the feeling of being accepted and of being able to associate with other people. Oftentimes, however, recognition from others is thwarted only by the standards that man must use for evaluating his own worth. There is a desire to express and exemplify the virtues of courage, truth, loyalty, kindness, and sympathy as well as an urge to show concern for others. Man, for the most part, wants to give of himself and his possessions. By giving, he feels that his companions will hold him in higher regard. It is a kind of reciprocating mores of society. One hand washes the other kind of custom.

Man's need to love and be loved may temporarily be so strong that the other needs, such as food and sleep, become secondary or of minor importance. The emotions of fear, hate, and jealousy may run rampant within the individual deprived of basic fulfillment. Similarly, being able to satisfy these needs gives him some happiness and makes life worthwhile for himself and his loved ones. However, there was a man who has demonstrated the greatest love for all humanity. "Greater love hath no man, than this, that a man lay down his life for his friends" (Jn. 15:13).

There are many other examples of love throughout the history of the human race, which I would not be able to address at this time. Permit me, however, to highlight just a few extraordinary examples of unconditional love. Take, for example, the love that Abraham had for God. He was willing to offer his only son Isaac as a living sacrifice to his Lord (Gen. 22:1–16). This demonstration of love, however, is a true representation of Christ. His was willing to lay down his life as a living sacrifice for us all!

In Matthew 22:35–40, we read of a lawyer, a Pharisee man, who asked Jesus a question, tempting him and saying, "Master, which is the greatest commandment in the law? Jesus said unto him, Thou shalt love the Lord thy God with all thy heart, and with all thy soul, and with all thy mind. This is the first and greatest commandment. And the second is like unto it, Thou shalt love thy neighbor as thyself. On these two commandments hang all the law and the prophets" (Matt. 22:36–40).

This extraordinary act of love by our Savior is the greatest demonstration of love throughout eternity!

> *Lord, dismiss us with thy blessing,*
> *Hope and comfort from above;*
> *Let us each, thy peace possessing,*
> *Triumph in redeeming love.*
>
> —Robert Hawker (1753-1827)

Despite men's best effort and quest for love, no one can outlove the Lord ever!

Aristotle

Aristotle (384–322 BC) was a Greek philosopher. He studied under Plato and later tutored Alexander the Great at the Macedonian court in 335 BC. According to historian, he opened a school in the Athenian Lyceum. During the anti-Macedonian agitation, after Alexander's death, Aristotle fled (323 BC) to Chalcis where he died. It is a grim reminder to us all that the inevitability of death is no respecter of person. His extant writings, largely in the form of lecture notes made by his students, include the *Organum* (treatises on logic), physics, *Metaphysics*, *De Anima* (On the Soul), *Nicomachean Ethics* and Eudemian Ethics, *Politics*, *De Poetica, Rhetoric*, and works on biology and physics.

The systematic use of philosophy held by Aristotle is discerning. Logic, as expressed in deductive argument, consists of two premises and conclusion self-evident, changeless first principles that form the basis of all knowledge. He taught that knowledge of a thing requires an inquiry into casualty and that the final cause, the purpose or function of the things, is primary. The highest good for the individual is the complete exercise of the specifically human function of rationality. By contrast, the Platonic belief that a concrete reality partakes of a form, but does not embody it. The Aristotelian system holds that, with the exception of the Prime Mover (God), form has no separate existence but is imminent in matter. Aristotle's work was lost following the decline of Rome but was reintroduced to the West through the work of Arab and Jewish scholars, becoming the basis of medieval scholasticism.

However noble the aspiration to achieve knowledge, *scholasticism* is not the ways and means to abundant life. In the book of Job, we read, "They spend their days in wealth, and in a moment go down to the grave. Therefore they say unto God, Depart from us; for we desire not the knowledge of thy ways. What is the Almighty, that we should serve him? and what profit should we have, if we pray unto him?" (Job 21:13–15). The truth is, there is every reason in the world to serve him. Angels bowed before him! Heaven and earth adore him! What a mighty God we serve! John, in the book of Revelation, was inspired to write of the elders in heaven, "And they rest not day and night, saying, Holy, holy,

holy, Lord God Almighty, which was, and is, and is to come… Thou art worthy, O Lord, to receive glory and honour and power: for thou hast created all things, and for thy pleasure they are, and were created" (Rev. 4:8,11). The answers given to the above questions, What is the Almighty that we should serve him? are found in Revelation 4:8–12.

The prophesies of the Scripture are being fulfilled all around us and in other parts of the world. As recent as August 1999 in Turkey, a very deadly earthquake took so many lives. A poignant question was asked in the headline of the leading news media, "Why, God? Why?" With all due respect, the answer can be found throughout the Scripture, most notably in Matthew 24:7–51. These are signs of the times, "and there shall be famines, and pestilences, and earthquakes, in divers places. All these are the beginning of sorrows" (Matt. 24:7–8).

Signs of the Times

The signs of the time are also referred to in Luke. "And great earthquakes shall be in divers places, and famines, pestilences; and fearful sights and great signs shall there be from heaven" (Lk. 21:11). "And there shall be signs in the sun, in the moon, and in the stars; and upon the earth distress of nations, with perplexity; the sea and the waves roaring" (Lk. 21:25).

The time to serve him is now! Despite life's awful tragedy, God is still a loving and a merciful God! There are those, however, who will continue to search for the answer, concerning the love of God in the midst of all the tragedies of life. An answer they are not likely to receive because God is not obligated to satisfy the curiosity of man's quest, only to seek and discover something odd or original.

Y2K

As we enter the twenty-first century and beyond, we are more likely to see many of the end times prophecy of the Bible be fulfilled in our day with great veracity. Therefore, let no one deceive you as to the day of our Lord's return. Jesus said, "But of that day and hour knoweth no man, no, not the angels of heaven, but my Father only" (Matt. 24:36).

The prophesies in Matthew 24, Luke 21:10–11, and Daniel 9:23–27 must be fulfilled. The fulfillment of prophecy should not be so alarming to Bible-believing Christians. After all, it should be unmistakably plain to us that the seventieth week of Daniel's prophecy is in its final stage of fulfillment.

11

THE INCREASE OF KNOWLEDGE

It was prophesied in the book of Daniel, almost three thousand years ago (570–536 or 586–536 BC) that in the last days, knowledge would increase. Without question, we are now living in the last days of Daniel's prophecy.

Just think of how far we have come since those predictions. From the time of Daniel; when chariot and horse was the fastest means of transportation, to the wooden ships propelled by both oars and sails; also used by the Vikings that carried Leif Erikson to America. The introduction of the mariner's compass aided Christopher Columbus and other explorers of the New World in the building and navigation of ships. Building wooden ships became an important industry, especially in Britain and the United States. Later, the steamship replaced the sailing ship and steel replace wood, which resulted in the construction of much larger ships. The steam engine was followed by the steam turbine and then diesel engine early in the twentieth century. In the 1950s, nuclear marine engines were introduced. Although the airplane has led to the virtual demise of the great ocean liner, luxurious cruise ships continue to be built. The pivotal vessels of modern warfare are the aircraft carrier and the submarine, but any sizable navy still includes destroyers, cruisers, and frigates.

The railroad is a form of transportation commonly consisting of steel rails called tracks on which powered locomotives draw freight cars and other rolling stocks. Other types of railroads, including monorails whose cars travel along a single rail pulled by horses along wooden rails, was used for mining purposes as early as the sixteenth century. The modern railroad, however, began with the steam locomotives pioneered by the Englishmen Richard Trevithick and George Stephenson in the early 1800s. Competition from other sources led to the decline of U.S. railroads beginning in the 1920s. After World War II, railroad companies claimed annual deficits in passenger service. Their plight was dramatized when the Penn Central Transportation Company filed for bankruptcy in 1970. In that same year, congress acted to create Amtrak, a public agency that took over all intricate passenger service in the U.S., which led the federal government to set up the Consolidated Rail Corporation (Conrail) system to operate six bankrupt railroads in the Northeast. Conrail was privatized in 1987. High-speed passenger trains, such as the bullet and TGV trains, were developed in Japan, France, and Germany. Magnetic levitation has also been run experimentally on short tracks in several countries.

Henry Ford, an American industrialist and pioneer automobile manufacture, was working as a machinist and engineer with the Edison Company. In his spare time, he built his first automobile in 1892. In 1903, he founded the Ford Motor Company. In 1908, he designed the Model T. Over fifteen million cars were sold before the model was discontinued in 1928 and a new design, Model A, was created to meet the growing competition.

The airplane is a heavier-than-air vehicle mechanically driven and fitted with fixed wings to support flight. On December 17, 1903, Americans Orville and Wilbur Wright flew the first airplane near Kitty Hawk, North Carolina. The machine was a biplane with two propellers chain-driven by a gasoline motor. Modern airplanes are monoplanes (one set of wings). Airplanes were classified as driven by jet propulsion or rocket. The airplane has six main parts: fuselage, wings, stabilizer, rudder, one or more engines, and landing gear. The fuselage is the main body, usually streamlined in form. The wings are the main supporting surfaces.

All these things, Daniel may have seen in his vision of the end times. Just think how fascinating it would have been just to see his reaction to the things he has seen. If we here in the United States of America, the most technologically advanced country in the world, are so awestruck by the launching of spaceships to the moon, the space shuttle, and other missions into outer space from Cape Canaveral. It is not surprising, however, to read of his reaction to his vision of the end times. We are now witnessing the proliferation of modern invention through the increase of knowledge in these last days. Daniel was horrified by his vision to the point that he fainted. The Lord strengthened him, instructed him to pen the book of his prophetic vision, and told him that the vision was not for his time. Therefore, it behooves us to take recognize the time we are living in. We are living in the last days of Daniel's prophecy. Let us be cognizant of the fact that if we, who are now living in the twenty-first century, are such curious spectators. So is it not unreasonable to expect Daniel to react in the manner in which he did. Why should we expect anything less exciting of Daniel in his day and age?

Vacuum Tube Paved the Way to High Technology

The invention of the triode vacuum tube in 1915 by Lee de Forest ushers the beginning of the revolution in information technology we enjoy today.

Before this time, the performance of the telephone network was constrained by electromagnetic and mechanical devices. Nationwide, the practicality of telephone calls was almost prohibitive. The calculated requirement for copper wires was about 0.5 to an inch in diameter. As required, the telephone network in New York City needed 90-foot poles with about 50 cross-arms and 12 wires per arm along the entire length of Broadway. Can you imagine the eyesore it must have been? Broadcast radio and TV were also fundamentally impossible to realize, and all had to await the arrival of the electronic amplifier and oscillator. Despite their best effort to harness the generation of radio carrier signals through rotating machinery, it was clear that something fundamentally new was required.

Here comes the vacuum tube to the rescue. Vacuum tube had an immediate impact on the long lines of telephone network and saw the establishment of radio services late in 1919. The very first two-way telephone communication between the USA and UK was in 1926 from the T&T Manhattan office to the post office in London. The regular public transatlantic service started in 1927 using High Frequency Radio with twelve channels. This was only eclipsed in 1956 by [TATI]—the first Trans-Atlantic Telephone cable with an initial thirty-six simultaneous speech circuits. HF Radio already provided twenty-four channels and cost of call was about half week wage. By 1986, there were 7UK [To USA] cables with a total of 12,000 speech circuits, and six satellites providing 57,000 circuits. At the time, TAT-8 was installed. The technology had moved on to fiber optics with 7,680 base circuits in one cable. Today systems are being planned with thousand-fold the capacity of TAT-8 and five million-fold that of TATI.

Transistor Revolution

Transistors are electronic devices used as a voltage and current amplifier consisting of semiconductor materials that share common physical boundaries. Transistors are an essential component of integrated circuits. They are used in many applications, including radio receivers, electronic computers, and automatic control instrumentation in space flight and guided missiles, etc. Since the American physicists, John Bardeen, Walter H. Brattain, and William Shockley, announced the invention of transistor in 1948, many types have been designed.

SIMEON W. JOHNSON

Integrated Circuit

Integrated circuits are miniature electronic circuits containing large numbers of electronic devices—including transistors, resistors, capacitors, and diodes—packaged as a single unit with leads extending from it for input, output, and power supply connections. Integrated circuits are used as computer memory circuits and microprocessors, In addition, they are categorized according to the number of transistors or other active circuit devices they contain. An ordinary or small-scale integrated circuit (SSI) may contain a large amount of such devices; a medium-scale integrated circuit (MSI) may contain several hundred; a large-scale integrated circuit (LSI), several hundred to a few thousand; an extra-large-scale integrated circuit (ELSI), a few thousand or more; and a huge-scale integrated circuit (VLSI), several hundred thousand or more. The first VSLI device was introduced in 1981.

In 1947, Shockley, Bardeen, and Brattain invented the transistor, and although the physics are fundamentally different, many of the concepts first pioneered by de Forest are evident. But, most importantly, the electronics markets test and measure and process technologies to make this invention possible were established by thirty-two years of prior vacuum tube developments. Today, vacuum tubes are rare. In stark contrast, ten thousand transistors are being manufactured for every man, woman, and child on the planet today with more than sixteen billion microprocessors to be imbedded in almost every device used in the developed world.

It is difficult to understate the impact of Lee de Forest and his groundbreaking discoveries and invention. Likewise, it is hard to imagine a world without his invention. There would be no radio and TV, only silent movies. There would be no telephones, no cell phones, and no computers. "No computer?" you may asked. Without the demands from telephone and radio broadcasting networks, we would not have developed vacuum tubes to the degree of perfection they reached today, nor would we have seen the transistor, integrated circuit, or an effective computer industry. There would no coaxial cables, optical fibers, lasers, microwave radio, satellites, or the entire modern conveniences that are necessary for our way of life today. We would be living similar lives to that of the early pioneers! Try to imagine yourself being without these thing—that is, the kind of antiquated way of life we would be living today—had they not invented and improved the vacuum tubes technology.

In summation, American inventor Lee de Forest improved the vacuum tubes by introducing a third electrode in 1906, which made modern radio possible. He called it the "Audion." He patented his tube in 1907 and presented the first live opera broadcast. In 1910, radio broadcast was born, but the public was not interested. Mr. de Forest sold the rights to the tube to American Telephone and Telegraph Company (now AT&T Corp.) for $390,000. Vacuum tubes became the essential components of all radio, telephone, radar, TV, and computer systems before the invention of the transistor in 1947.

Relief versus Stress

Although these modern high-tech devices are designed to facilitate life through their use by reducing the stress level of everyday chore, it is true that these modern conveniences, while improving the lives of many, has also greatly increased the anxiety and stress levels of others somewhat.

Think of how far we have come since the time of Daniel's prediction compared to today's modern time. In Daniel's time, the fastest means of transportation were chariots and horses. Today, we have spacecraft and rocket ships that can travel many times faster than the speed of sound, which is approximately 750 miles per hour.

What's Looming on the Horizon?

In our lifetime, we have witnessed the advance in science through cutting-edge technology at an astonishing rate. Animals cloning is no longer taboo, with the possibility of human cloning and a host of other possibilities. Controlling your home from wherever there is a telephone will be the in thing of the future. This is the direction we are heading in reference to the prophetic increase of knowledge prophesied in Daniel 12:4 in the last days.

With a state-of-the-art speech-recognition software, HAL2000 gives you control of almost everything in your home with a simple voice command. They are talking true voice-activated automation, not the voice-prompt architecture that does the talking for you! With HAL2000 on your PC and standard X-10 modules, say the word and your wish is Hal's command. Close your blinds, ask what the temperature is at your home, and start your car on those bitter cold mornings—just say the words. Everything you can think of is on the drawing board at the designing and production stage for the future, some of those things are not yet conceivable to most of us.

How amazing it is to see all of the consumer electronics technologies we never could have imagined or ever dreamed of becoming reality! First, as prototypes, then as very expensive consumer products, and then as consumer products most of us can afford. It's not practical for me to mention all of the innovative, high-tech consumer and industrial products available to us today and other developed countries of the world. However, many others are not so fortunate. In spite of man's accomplishments, however, his finite ability will never be equal to the only true God, the Creator of heaven and earth and the universe in its entity. "To whom then will ye liken God? or what likeness will you compare unto him?" (Isa. 40:18). There is no equal.

From the time of Daniel's prophecy, the increase of knowledge in the last days compared to when there were only chariots and horses and ships that sail with oars to steamships, railroad cars, Henry Ford Model T cars, airplanes, the development of the vacuum tube, transistors, integrated circuits, and satellite communications! We have come a long way, haven't we?

Satellite Communication

Satellites orbit the earth around the equator at a distance of 22,300 miles or 35,860 kilometers A satellite rotates around the earth in exactly twenty-four hours, precisely in synchronism with the Earth and appears to be fixed or stationary. Thus, the term *synchronous* or *geostationary orbit* is coined. Typical rotational periods range from approximately one and a half hours for a 100-mile height to twenty-four hours for a 22,300-mile height. The speed varies depending upon the distance of the satellite from the Earth. For a circular orbit, the speed is constant; for an elliptical orbit, the speed varies depending on the height. Low-orbiting satellites of about a hundred miles height have a speed of 17,500 miles per hour. Very high satellites, such as communications satellites, that have a height of approximately 22,300 miles, rotate much slower at a typical speed of 6,800 miles per hour.

All of the modern conveniences we enjoy today came about as a direct result of the triode vacuum tube invention in 1915 by Lee de Forest, which ushered the beginning of the technological revolution we take for granted today. With the increase in knowledge and understanding, there is a range of information by the product as a result of being educated. Such knowledge can be dangerous if not used to the glory of God! For that reason, we should take heed to the word of God who warns, "Woe unto them that are wise in their own eyes, and prudent in their own sight" (Isa. 5:21).

Intellectual Geniuses

Admittedly, there are many intellectual geniuses in the world today with above-average intelligence and higher-than-normal IQs. There are others with unusual ability to communicate by means of extrasensory perception (ESP) or mental telepathy. They reasoned that if thoughts were transferred from one mind to another without the usual means of communication or use of any of the sensory clues, then man must produce mental power.

That, however, would be a fearful thing. "For God has not given us the spirit of fear; but of power, and of love, and of a sound mind" (2 Tim. 1:7). The thought of man having the ability to read each other's mind is a fearful thought. God has given us faith, wisdom, knowledge, understanding, and a free will to choose, but the will to read each other's thought is not his will for man. The kind of thought that the Father has in mind for us is found in Philippians 2:3–5, "Let nothing be done through strife or vainglory; but in lowliness of mind, let each esteem others better than themselves. Let this mind be in you, which was also in Christ Jesus."

According to psychologists, a person may be able to turn fifteen cards and predict 100 percent what is coming up to do no better than the laws of chance would predict on the next fifteen. However, the omniscient Creator of all things is always perfect in his predictions. There are some geniuses with high IQs over 200, some of these people happen to be astronomers who are able to measure the distance of faraway stars within our galaxy. Proximal Centauri, the closest star to Earth, is at a distance of 4.3 light-years away. Therefore, according to scientific calculation, light traveling at the speed of 180,000 miles per second would move approximately 25.8 trillion miles in 4.3 light-years. However, no one has or will ever be able to calculate the speed of the fastest medium of travel in the world and the universe—our thoughts! Therefore, can anyone honestly claim, they can truly measure the speed of thought?

Whether you are a genius with an IQ of over 200 or an imbecile with an IQ below 70, man's device cannot measure the speed of your God-given thoughts by the use of the bell curve classification or by any other means.

12

THE SIGNIFICANCE OF THE SPEED OF THOUGHT

The idea that conveys to mind pertaining to the significance of the speed of thought is mind-boggling. Try to imagine for a moment how fast the speed of thought really is. Over the years, astronauts and astronomers have been frantically exploring space, *our new frontier,* looking for life on other planets. Hypothetically speaking, in the event, they should ever find life on other planets and succeed in their quest for other forms of life with extraterrestrial intelligence, other questions need answers, such as how would they communicate with each other? Would they depend solely on the physical limitations of the speed of light traveling at the rate of 186,000 miles per second? That is a distance of approximately 25.8 trillion miles. That is a very slow process compared to the speed of thought. When all one has to do right now, is just think of being anywhere in the world or the universe and your thought takes you there instantly, faster than the speed of light.

For more information of the significance of the speed of thought, let us refer to the author of absolute truth found in Revelation chapters 1 through 22, which gives us both vivid and spiritual description of the difference between spiritual reality and natural perception of the speed of thought. The natural person can only perceive in his or her mind, unlike John who had eyewitness account of the difference between natural perception and spiritual reality. John bears record of this fact as he was transformed from the natural into the supernatural realm where he observed things both in heaven and on earth in a manner our natural minds can only perceive as fast as or faster than the speed of thought.

The Revelation of Saint John the Divine

Saint John the divine reveals "The Revelation of Jesus Christ, which God gave unto him, to shew unto his servants things which must shortly come to pass; and he sent and signified it by his angel unto his servant John: Who bear record of the word of God, and the testimony of Jesus Christ, and of all things that he saw" (Rev. 1:1–2).

The things that John saw and heard cannot be trivialized or interpreted as symbolic revelation of make-believe events from one's imagination. For example, verses 1 and 2 gives us a vivid description of what John saw, "After this I looked, and, behold, a door was opened in heaven: and the first voice which I heard was as it were of a trumpet talking with me; which said, Come up hither, and I will shew thee things which must be hereafter. And immediately I was in the spirit; and, behold, a throne was set in heaven, and one sat on the throne" (Rev. 4:1–2). Take cognizance of John's absolute assurance of his supernatural transformation as the event unfolds.

In the natural way of thinking, one could only perceive in his mind to be there. On the other hand, in the spirit realm, John was there immediately, not thousands of light-years later, traveling at 186,000 miles per second. At that rate of speed, John would still be on his way to heaven. We know that God is patient and long-suffering, but not to that extent. Despite mankind's proud achievements, he has his limitations. Therefore, he can only perceive in his heart and thoughts by the natural laws of physics in order to communicate with inanimate man-made objects he launched to the moon, beyond the far reaches of outer space.

Arguably, the critics might scoff at the past and present discussion of John's experiences as science fiction and a figment of John's imagination. If that was the case, no one can argue against the significance of the speed of thought; that is, with the exception of the Spirit of God the Creator. There is not a faster medium of travel known to mortal man. If John's experiences was just a figment of his imagination, then he alone among mortals would have possessed the ability to simultaneously observe the things that he saw and heard in heaven and on earth as they unfold. Among the many things that John saw and heard are:

> *And every creature which is in heaven, and on the earth, and under the earth, and such as are in the sea, and all that are in them, heard I saying, Blessing, and honour, and glory, and power, be unto him that sitteth upon the throne, and unto the Lamb for ever and ever. And the four beasts said, Amen. And the four and twenty elders fell down and worshipped him that liveth forever and ever. (Rev. 5:13–14)*

Further evidence reveals many other spectacular revelations. "And I beheld when he had opened the sixth seal, and, lo, there was a great earthquake; and the sun became black as sackcloth of hair, and the moon became as blood" (Rev. 6:12). In conclusion of the extraordinary experiences of John's testimony at the closing of the book of Revelation 6:13–22). These are prophetic events revealed to John but by Divine revelation of the Spirit of Christ. Therefore, the difference between the significance of the speed of thought, and the figment of one's imagination, has clearly demonstrated the difference between natural perception of things and spiritual reality.

During 1957, scientists from sixty-six countries made special efforts to gather information about the Earth and space around us. "Russians Launch Earth Satellite" was the headline on October 4, 1957 that announced the Space Age. Despite man's best effort, who among us mortals is able to control the medium of thoughts? No one! Not one! Only the omniscient, all-knowing God of all creations can know the thoughts of men. "Thou knowest my downsitting and mine uprising, thou understandest my thoughts afar off. Thou compassest my path and my lying down, and art acquainted with all of my ways" (Ps. 139:2–3). "To whom then will ye liken God? or what likeness will ye compare unto him?" (Isa. 40:18). "To whom then will ye liken me, or shall I be equal? saith the Holy One" (Isa. 40:25).

Voyager 1 is the most distant man-made object in space. The space probe, to date, is the furthest man-made object at 10.4 billion kilometers (6.5 billion miles) from its home planet, NASA said. Traveling at 17.4 kilometers (10.8 miles) per second, *Voyager 1* is sending back data to Earth by means of nuclear-powered batteries. The probe has been traveling since September 5, 1997, when it was launched from the Kennedy Space Center in Cape Canaveral, Florida. It left our solar system at the staggering speed of 37,000 miles per hour many years ago. *Voyager 1* is now "so far from home that it takes nine hours and thirty-six minutes for a radio signal traveling at the speed of light to reach Earth," project director Ed Massey commented. "That signal, produced by a 20-watt radio transmitter, is so faint that the amount of power reaching our antennas is twenty billion times smaller than the power of a digital watch battery."

It doesn't take a rocket scientist to reasonably conclude that such faint signal strength cannot compete with the sound and voice of the God of all creations who spoke things into existence. He also spoke to John in the isle of Patmos and said, "Come up hither, and I will shew thee things which must be hereafter. And immediately I was in the spirit: and, behold, a throne was set in heaven, and one sat on the throne" (Rev. 4:1–2).

The arms of man are too short to box with God. While finite man is busy clenching his fists in the face of his Creator, God stands taller, and higher above finite man. Higher as the heaven is above the earth! Therefore, how can mortals fly into the face of God his Creator with a man-made object like *Voyagers 1* and *2*? Certainly not by radio, TV, and microwaves in the electromagnetic spectrum.

God is speaking to us through his written word and, in many ways, through a still small voice. However, at his Second Coming, his trumpet will sound so loud, it will wake up the dead. "For the Lord himself shall descend from heaven with a shout, with the voice of the archangel, and with the trump of God: and the dead in Christ shall rise first: Then we which are alive and remain shall be caught up together with them in the clouds to meet the Lord in the air: and so shall we ever be with the Lord. Wherefore comfort one another with these words" (1 Thess. 4:16–18). This is possible only if we abide in his word and his word abides in us. No one who is truly honest with himself, who does not abide in his word can take solace in these promises.

The Omniscience of God versus Man's Wisdom

Who among man would we compare to the all-knowing God? Certainly not Newton or Einstein. According to an article I read in a magazine recently, "Einstein once said of Newton that he was the most brilliant man that ever lived. He also said that if Newton had the same information he had, he would have reached the same conclusion."

The equation Einstein gave the world forced a revision of physical law and effects due to how famous it became: $e = me^2$, which means that the amount of energy in a body is equal to the mass of a body, many times the square of the velocity of light. The velocity of light is about 300,000,000 meters per second (or about 186,000 miles per second). Newton's law, by contrast, revised scientists' thinking.

1. *The law of inertia.* A body at rest tends to remain at rest, and a body in motion tends to continue to move along a straight line unless acted upon by an unbalanced force.
2. *The law of acceleration.* An unbalanced force acting on a body causes a body to accelerate in the direction of the unbalanced force, and the acceleration is directly proportional to the unbalanced force and inversely proportional to the mass of the body.
3. *The law of balanced forces.* For every action, there is an equal and opposite reaction.

From my observation of the article, it is obvious that God alone is all knowing. "Before me there was no God formed, neither shall there be after me" (Isa. 43:10).

The article goes on to say that there are only a few people in the world who really understand Newton and Einstein's scientific contributions. However, let the reader be the judge of that. The above statement that refers to the law of balance ("For every action, there is an equal and opposite reaction") tends to pose questions. Is there an equal and opposite reaction to the one who has measured the waters in the hollow of his hand? What force is equal in action and opposition to him who has created the heavens and the earth and all that dwell therein? Is there an equal force or reaction to the omnipotent Creator of the sun, the moon, and the billions of stars in our galaxy? The answer is a resounding no! Therefore, there is no equal and opposite reaction to this force.

EEPROM

As promised in the preceding chapters that I would try to elaborate on the function and use of the EEPROM function (electronically erasable program read-only memory). Allow me to take this opportunity to make good on my promise. The EEPROM is a small integrated component developed in the late seventies, commonly called an IC chip that controls various aspects of consumer electronics, mainly the late-model TV sets, PCs, and various electronics devices. It has a programmable read-only memory that can be erased usually by exposure to ultraviolet radiation.

This unique device is pivotal for the many crucial operations in whatever device it is embedded into. It is electronically programmable so you can read and write to its program electronically. Not so with ROM chips, which are permanently programmed in the IC software program. Do you recall what I have stated in my previous statements concerning the ROM that it is not user friendly? In other words, the ROM is designed for user not to alter its program. Recapping my previous statements of the EEPROM, a subject that is relevant in this regard, there is no comparison between the creative work of God and his written words (ROMW) described in Genesis chapters 1–3 and Revelation 22:18–21. "Thus saith the Lord."

Electronic Fingerprints versus God's Unfathomable Trail

Electronic fingerprints versus God's unfathomable trail is, without question, incomprehensible! It is written, "For my thoughts are not your thoughts, neither are your ways my ways, saith the Lord. For as the heavens are higher than the earth, so are my ways higher than your ways, and my thoughts than your thoughts" (Isa. 55:8–9).

Therefore, who among us can ascribe such awesome attributes to his or her character? Obviously, only the omniscient, all-knowing God can make such indisputable claims! Everything that mankind has ever done is recorded and has left its trail of evidence on recorded history by accountability to the authorities, not so with the Great I Am. He is exalted above all the heavens and the earth. His footstep is not known (Ps. 77:19). Us mortals, however, are accountable for everything we do.

For example, every person who has ever conducted electronic transactions or used computers has left electronic trails somewhere in the system, enabling the experts to trace its origin in case of fraudulent use or other misconducts. God's ways and attributes, on the other hand, are perfect and without flaws, therefore it has withstood the test of any negative scrutiny, which makes the interjection of read only my word (ROMW) applicable for this discussion. Man is accountable to God and other men for his or her actions. Whether good or bad, rich or poor, there is no exception. Thus, ROMW is a sharp contrast to EEPROM, a program that you can read to and erase at will, usually by exposure to ultraviolet radiation. God's word cannot be erased by any means. History is full with stories of man's futile attempts to eradicate and erase the word of God from the ancient of days even to the present time. To no avail, thank God.

Jesus emphatically declared, "For verily I say unto you, Till heaven and earth pass, one jot or one title shall in no wise pass from the law, till all be fulfilled" (Matt. 5:18). This is the confidence believers have in the unchanging word of God. Therefore, man's finite ability to fathom the wisdom of God or erase his written word is futile. Apostle Paul sums it up, "O the depth of the riches both of the wisdom and knowledge of God! how unsearchable are his judgments and his ways past finding out! For who hath known the mind of the Lord? or who hath been his counselor?" (Rom. 11:33–34).

In closing, in the eve of the New Millennium, year 2000, a TV anchorman interviewed America's most leading astrologer to give his analysis of what a millennium is in reference to time. He gave a descriptive analysis in comparison to the age of the universe as being over thirteen billion years old. A millennium is like one strand of a human hair in that regard. He was also asked if he could give his prediction on the Y2K crisis. He admitted that he could not. He goes on to say, however, that only astrologers can predict when, if, and where the sun is going to rise and set the next day. Such arrogant statement evoked a series of poignant questions.

Where were the astrologers when Earth was without form and void? Darkness was upon the face of the earth. "And God said, Let there be light: and there was light" (Gen. 1:3). A creative declaration by the omnipotent, omniscient Creator who is able to predict with precision how, when, and where the sun is going to be at any point in time. Where were the astrologers to make predictions during the course of events? Could the astrologers predict when and where the sun would appear during the forty days when it rained nonstop causing the great flood in Genesis 7:17? In addition, could they also predict the phenomena of the sun when it stood still for one day at the command of Joshua in Joshua 10:13? God allowed him to win the battle over the Amorites. Could the astrologers have predicted that a star would lead wise men to the place where Christ was born? Absolutely not! In Matthew 16:2–3, Jesus said to the Sadducees, "When it is evening, ye say, It will be fair weather: for the sky is red. And in the morning, It will be foul weather to day: for the sky is red and lowering. O ye hypocrites, ye can discern the face of the sky; but can ye not discern the signs of the times?"

On the other hand, men by nature are boasters of their achievement. Nevertheless, they are not able to discern the signs of the times. Despite man's ability and achievements in many areas, such as interstellar space exploration and charting the course of our solo systems and the stars, he is still limited in his ability to compete with the Creator of heaven and earth who has demonstrated the difference between spiritual reality and natural perception of the figment of imagination of one's thought. God is the one who spoke the earth and the universe into existence in the beginning of Creation until the end of all things described in the book of Revelation. In addition, the voice of the Lord said, "Come up hither, and I will shew thee things which must be hereafter, And immediately I was in the spirit: and, behold, a throne was set in heaven, and one sat on the throne" (Rev. 4:1–2). Immediately, John was in the presence of the Lord. It would take him a very long time to reach our closest star or even by the most advanced method of space travel known to us today. Just think of the time, restriction, and distance interstellar travel would impose. Therefore, there is no comparison between spiritual realities like John described in the book of Revelation and the figment of one's imagination.

In closing, the prophecy proclaimed from the beginning of time in the garden of Eden concerning the coming Messiah (Gen. 3:15) was fulfilled through the birth, death, burial, and resurrection of Christ our Savior.

"In the beginning was the Word, and the Word was with God, and the Word was God. The same was in the beginning with God. All things were made by him; and without him was not any thing made that was made. In him was light; and the life was the light of men. And the light shineth in darkness; and the darkness comprehended it not" (Jn. 1:1–5). Is there not overwhelming evidence presented in these stated facts?

> *That which was from the beginning, which we have heard, which we have seen with our eyes, which we have looked upon, and our hands have handled, of the Word of life; (For the life was manifested, and we have seen it, and bear witness, and*

show unto you that eternal life, which was with the Father, and was manifested unto us;) That which we have seen and heard declare we unto you, that ye also may fellowship with us: and truly our fellowship with the Father, and with his Son Jesus Christ. And these things write we unto you, that your joy may be full. This then is the message, which we have heard of him, and declare unto you, that God is, light, and in him is no darkness at all. (1 John 1:1–5)

Prophetic Proclamation Being Fulfilled

As it has been proclaimed and fulfilled, it will finally be completed. No one has or ever will be able to predict with such remarkable accuracy as the Bible has predicted. Finally, the declaration of creation declared the Genesis. "In the beginning God created the heaven and the earth" (Gen. 1:1) and end with "I am Alpha and Omega, the beginning and the end, the first and the last" (Rev. 22:13).

ABOUT THE AUTHOR

Simeon Johnson wrote his first book entitled, *A Myopic Life Resonated from the Brink of the Abyss*. This book is changing lives everywhere. He is not the author of a second book title *ROMW versus RAMB Reveals God, Adam, and Creation*.

Mr. Johnson graduated from National Technical School with a master's course in radio and TV electronics. He earned his FCC general radio telephone first class license, with radar endorsement. He currently lives in Stockbridge, Georgia.

"A life is a precious thing to waste!"

Born in rural Jamaica as the youngest of thirteen children, Simeon Johnson suffered the tragic loss of his beloved mother as an infant. As the youngest son of ten brothers and three sisters, it has been a very painful loss for me at such an early age in my childhood. Nevertheless, that did not thwart my God-given ability to pull myself up by my bootstrap after being raised by my youngest sister. Thank heaven for much fortitude that enables me to have a significant amount of mental gymnastics. I have overcome all the odds of that tragic loss so early in my life.

The general knowledge I acquired through perseverance and my passionate love and zest for knowledge reassures me that being a self-taught person, nothing is impossible with God! Further studies enabled me to graduate from American School high school in Chicago Illinois with an academic diploma. Through correspondence in a master course in radio and TV electronics, I earned my FCC general radio telephone first class license with radar endorsement. My intense passion and desire for knowledge, which will last forever, has inspired me to increase my overall knowledge and broaden my horizon from adult phonics to speed-reading, mega memory learning, and the latest photo reading course. I currently live and work in New York City.

On the eve of the new millennium on December 31, 1999, admittedly a very exuberant moment in my life, I got to see Daniel's prophecy fulfilled. Right before my own eyes, I witnessed the consortium of the cutting edge technology simultaneously displayed around the world! An estimated six billion inhabitants were well represented as I watched the events unfolded on worldwide TV. Thank God!

In addition, thank you, Mother, for the precious gift of life. I have overcome and lived to see these events unfold. For these reasons, I was inspired to add to the title of my book. What would Adam and Eve say if they could see us now?

www.ingramcontent.com/pod-product-compliance
Lightning Source LLC
Chambersburg PA
CBHW021428070526
44577CB00001B/115